Oh Myyy!

THERE GOES THE INTERNET

GEORGE TAKEI

ISBN-13 (U.S. Edition): 978-0615775371

Oh Myyy! Limited Liability Company
1501 Broadway, Suite 2900, New York, NY 10036
1-917-720-3289 | www.theohmybook.com

Originally published in digital edition by
Oh Myyy! Limited Liability Company, November 2012

Contents

Dedicated to

my husband Brad Takei,
who swore I had it in me
to write another book

and to

my trusty interns,
who demanded
not to be named.

Preface

Friends, much has happened in the fast-paced world of Social Media since first releasing this book in digital form back in November of 2012. When the influential website *mashable.com* named its ten most influential people on Facebook for 2012, imagine my shock to see my name topping that list! Fans flooded my wall with congratulations, many pointing out that my page had beat out Barack Obama and God, who apparently maintains His own page. Oh myyy, indeed.

But I really can't take credit for that honor. As I've always maintained, it is the community of dedicated fans on my page that makes it such a vibrant and engaging place. As I write this, the numbers have grown to nearly 4 million. More importantly, some 4-5 million people per week check in with the page, either liking, commenting or sharing, resulting in a "reach" that has climbed as high as 80 million people. Facebook has also improved the way I can interact with fans, with a new feature that allows me to reply directly to fan comments, and a layout that features "top" comments first, rewarding those that receive the most "likes." There is now a very amusing contest with each post to see which fan might provide the funniest or most insightful response.

What pleases me most, however, is that my Facebook page and my Twitter account have become a launching ground for promoting awareness and effecting change. For example, in March when a pair of Marriage Equality cases went before the U.S. Supreme Court, I asked fans to join with me in turning Facebook red. By this I meant changing our Facebook profiles for two days to a red "equal" sign, in solidarity with the Human Rights Campaign's equality logo. I was astounded and humbled when over 70,000 fans, gay and straight, followed suit, creating a wave of support across the Internet as millions of their friends took up the cause. For the first time in history, there was a virtual "march" of epic proportions that surprised even the most cynical of the digerati.

Of course, we couldn't do this without adding a bit

of fun. Coincident with the campaign was the rise of a new and omnipresent meme, Tardar the Grumpy Cat, whose characteristic "No" was replaced that day with a startlingly different message:

But some things haven't changed. I still rely nearly exclusively on my own fans to provide most of the entertainment, with me acting merely a conduit for their humor. The difference now is that it isn't un-common for fan-shared posts to reach over 100,000

"likes" each, especially if it evokes a collective nostalgia for a song or a beloved character from television or film.

In short, my forays in social media have only but begun. No one really knows where it will all go from here, but I do know this: wherever it is, we will boldly go, together.

<u>Oh Myyy!</u>

How in the world did a common, everyday exclamation come to be so associated with me? "Oh My!" truly has become my signature. Many people ask me about when I started saying it, but it's actually something I'd been using all my life. "Oh my!" Doesn't everybody say it? "Oh my!" Now, somehow, it's become my brand. For this, I put the blame squarely on one world-renowned rascal named Howard Stern.

I had been on Howard Stern's radio show many times since the early 90s — a few times intentionally, but more often not. The times I purposefully appeared were to promote a play I was in or the publication of my autobiography, *To the Stars*. But more frequently, I'd been "on" because of bandit recordings. Once, Howard surreptitiously recorded me while on the phone with a celebrity imitator pretending, absurdly, to be Ricardo Montalban.

Howard Stern has had his fun with me, and his listeners seemed to be having a hilarious good time listening to his mischief at my expense. I got points for being a good sport, I suppose. The Stern Show techies even spliced my voice from the audiocassette version of my autobiography and manipulated the words to make it seem like I was uttering outrageously obscene statements. They claim they did all this because they love me, but I must say, I've never been loved in such a bizarre fashion.

Howard also seemed to have fallen in love with me saying "Oh my!" whenever he said or did something outrageous, like when he asked one voluptuous young woman on his show to take her bra off. "Oh my!" What else could I say? It was even more apt when she did. "Oh my!" indeed. Howard, for some unfathomable reason, thought my reflexive "Oh my!" was hilarious. So he played a recording of it over and over again — even when I wasn't on the show. I thought it was silly, but it was also admittedly quite droll.

I first realized "Oh my!" was becoming personally linked with me when I went on a national book tour for *To the Stars*. Young men who had patiently stood in line for my autograph would slip the book toward me with roguishly insinuating smiles and ask me to sign it with "Oh my!" I knew right away they were Howard Stern fans and realized then that it had become my signature phrase.

"Oh my!" goes beyond a response of amusement or surprise. It is also an expression of awe and wonder. Our world is full of amazing phenomena: a stunningly rapturous sunrise, a night sky spangled with stardust, the fiery beauty of a volcanic lava flow. They all merit a "Oh my!" Humankind's imagination and innovation is truly breathtaking. Today we take for granted technology that was mere science fiction just over four decades ago on *Star Trek*. I am a 75-year old man who grew up transported by adventures I experienced with my ears glued to the radio. When black and white television was introduced, that was a sensational "Oh my!" event. We could see a movie on a round screen in a box in our own living room. What a groundbreaking invention!

Our dazzling tech-driven society today stimulates and inspires me. We have become instantaneously interconnected, not only with other people of this earth, but with far-off planets. A robot we created is now roving the surface of Mars and sending back photos to us on Earth — what an amazing achievement. I want to revel in and enjoy this "Oh my!" world —

so much so, that I've begun to accentuate the very phrase. As we all know, the addition of a few Ys adds a certain *je ne sais quoi*. "Hey" simply doesn't quite carry the same suggestive appeal in a text message as the more inviting "Heyyy." And with that, "Oh myyy!" was born.

As many a fan has posted on my Facebook wall,

© *skala,* © *fotografie4you.eu,* © *Alexey Gnezdilov - Fotolia.com*
Used with Permission

Don't worry, it took me a while to get this, too.

Status Symbolism

Social media depends on the act of sharing. "Duh," you say. But what is less clear is *why* we choose to share things through our social networks. Sure, we want to keep our friends and families current, particularly when something significant happens. "I got a job promotion." "I'm a mom again." "I need bail money." But that hardly scratches the surface of our modern sharing rituals.

Once upon a time, we had to call or write to everyone we knew with such news. More dutiful friends shared an annual family photo and penned lengthy, form Christmas letters, complete with a "Dear X" salutation (likely filled in by hand in textbook cursive) and a yearly summary of their notable achievements and news (usually in hard-to-read italic typeset on even harder-to-read blue or red paper). Those chestnuts are rather scarce now in this age of status posting. Perhaps those same people today could simply email a holiday greeting with a link to their Facebook Timelines, all major Life Events carefully laid out, each album informatively and accurately titled, each photo auto-enhanced with red-eye removed.

But beyond important news, let's face it: Facebook and Twitter are filled with information no one really needs to know. "At the gym." "Ate donuts for dinner." "Got shingles."

It's harder to understand why people post this information, and admittedly harder still to understand why we continue to devour it on a daily basis. We post in the sincere hope of providing others a more honest and open sense of who we are, from the very special moments to the mundane. Sharing is an act of trust, for ridicule is an ever-present risk on the Internet today. But I've recently concluded that sharing is also often an act of deception. More on that later.

On a deeper level, the sharing of our lives on a daily basis is a statement of our values and of what makes us tick. In so doing, friends who are far away may feel close by, and long lost acquaintances or relationships may resurface, often with alarming results.

Monique
I hope Mrs. Johanson is at the reunion, she was the best teacher/my favorite of all of CHS!

Like · Comment · Share · 7 minutes ago via iOS ·

👍 10 people like this.

> **Thomas** YAYA!! I had her too!
> 3 minutes ago · Like
>
> **Larry** WTF that lady was youre favorite teacher?!? she a bitch cuz of her i had 2 take summer school!!
> 2 minutes ago · Like
>
> **Johanson** Sadly, I will not be able to attend, but thank you all for inviting me to the group. Larry, I am sorry you feel that way. Obviously my grammar lessons didn't stick too well.
> 2 minutes ago · Like
>
> **Jack** LMFAO! BURN!!! GO MRS J!!!!
> about a minute ago · Like
>
> **Larry** w/ever i couldnt say it n hs so i say it now U R A BITHC!
> about a minute ago · Like
>
> **Johanson** Larry, you can barely say it now. Also, you could have said that in High School, because "BITHC" isn't a real word. I am going to use my context clues and assume you are attempting to call me a bitch. In that case, I will point out that your facebook information lets me know that you are currently single and unemployed. Who is the bitch now?
> a few seconds ago · Like · 👍 1

It is easy to underestimate the impact our hyper-connectivity has upon us as individuals and on the human species in general. We are naturally social creatures, but at least until recently our social interactions were limited to those we saw, spoke to, worked with, and slept with (or stopped sleeping with) daily. In the networked world, there are fewer Eleanor Rigbys to sing about, for even the loneliest among us can venture out with relative anonymity and find solace in the comfort of others' lives, particularly if those lives appear equally mundane. By the way, if you don't know who Eleanor Rigby is, you probably were born after 1985 and need to listen to some real music.

There is a voyeuristic quality to it all as well. Before we had Facebook, we began our obsession with reality television, where we followed the lives of complete strangers and watched their dramas unfold, breathless with anticipation for the next meltdown. Smartly edited by experienced producers, these shows made television audiences feel as if they had been invited into someone else's world. And here's the rub: by witnessing the rawness of the emotions, on full display for us all to take in, these "real" people felt like our colleagues, our friends, our families.

Facebook and Twitter started out like poorly funded cable access reality shows, running 24/7 with limited but ever-increasing commercial interruption. But instead of seeing the daily drama of strangers, we reveled in the streaming peeks into the lives of those we actually knew, one finger pressed firmly on the pulses of their existence. It became easier than ever to compare our own lives to theirs, and to see if the grass really was greener.

But things morphed quickly on Facebook due to a little button called "like." The only real way we could tell whether anyone cared about what we did was if friends hit that button. Our Facebook experience became, as they say, "game-ified." Rather quickly, the savvier "producers" among us began to edit and present their lives to achieve more "likes". Instead of a moment-to-moment transparent view, we began to receive the edited docudrama. Popularity in the Facebook schoolyard could be measured in thumbs-ups — or more recently, the more difficult-to-value number of "subscribers." For many hapless users, their own lives began to appear dull, or worse still, not like-worthy, when stacked against the smart, glamorous and Instagram-filtered vacations of friends and colleagues. All of life's insecurities, long ago tucked safely away after years of wisdom or expensive therapy, welled right back up again with each page refresh.

In short, social media soon became more about being media savvy, and less about being social. Hollywood caught on quickly. Celebrities and their handlers began to use social media to open carefully constructed windows into their lives — enough to titillate but not really enlighten. Fans followed, hoping for bits of insight and, if lucky, the occasional hastily tweeted, then suddenly retracted, outburst.

19

> The reason we struggle
> with insecurity is
> because we compare
> our behind the scenes
> with everyone else's
> highlight reel.
> — Steve Furtick

But this was just a commercial reflection of a growing social phenomenon. Indeed, when you think about it, on a broader level each of us now makes the decisions of a celebrity. With each post or tweet, we choose what to keep private and what to make public, what face to show the world and what to keep buried. It is a kind of deception, and we have become reality stars, every one of us.

Speaking from personal experience, having *any* social media presence followed by thousands or even millions of people is not for the faint of heart; one drunken tweet or post, and the gig is up. I've unintentionally shared pictures meant for a select group of friends that, to my horror, went out to tens of thousands of fans before I could delete them. Oh myyy, indeed.

Facebook wised up and started permitting "filters" — privacy settings that one had to master like a second language. Friends and family were divided into those who could know everything, some things, or almost nothing. Each post thereafter carried with it a critical decision: Make public (and get the most attention), or limit severely (and save your dignity). There are many who have simply refused to apply such filters and are living their lives out publicly and unabashedly — what I call the "Lindsay Lohan Effect." We love these people. We really do.

Apart from the privacy concerns, I decided a while back that my life simply wasn't interesting enough on a day-to-day level to update others in real time. No one would really care to know what I ate for breakfast or which movie I went to see — and if they did, I really didn't want them commenting about it. Instead, I set out simply to share with my fans many of the funny or inspiring things I came across. What I didn't realize at the time was that, by sharing these posts, I could grow a whole community that didn't exist before.

It started, of course, with science fiction fans, especially long-time Trekkies who were happy to experience some kind of regular contact with Mr. Sulu. I owe my career to these fans, and I have never understood actors who don't take the time to acknowledge and thank them. On Twitter and Facebook, I soon learned I could go one step further and actually interact with fans everyday. One of my earliest posts on Twitter garnered much attention and basically launched my online journey:

 George Takei ✓
@GeorgeTakei

I broke that Asian driver stereotype by being the best helmsman in the galaxy.

← Reply   ⟲ Retweet   ★ Favorite

Fans seemed genuinely surprised and delighted that a man of my, let's say, "maturity" would get himself a Twitter account and start putting it out there. I recall gaining thousands of fans in a single day and being at the top of the Twitter homepage for a few short but glorious hours. And I must say, for the first month it was all pretty much fun and games, with humorous posts about current events and my own odd take on them. That all changed one fateful day in March of 2011, when I was awakened by a friend who alerted me to the tragedy of the Japanese earthquake and tsunami. That was the first time I learned the true value and power of the social network: an open channel of communication that can not only entertain but also unite us in a common cause, from responding to a disaster to — as the Arab Spring showed us — toppling a government.

That morning, as I witnessed the extent of the devastation in Japan, I put out the following tweet, in the hopes of raising money for disaster relief:

 **George Takei** ✓
@GeorgeTakei

Today we are all Japanese. Give $10 to help. Text REDCROSS to 90999, or click http://ow.ly/4ctzx Pls RT!

← Reply ⭐ Retweet ⭐ Favorite

That simple plea, sent out to my modest fan-base of some 30,000 mostly *Star Trek* followers, echoed and reverberated beyond all expectation. Celebrities took up the call, retweeting it to their fans and thus around the world in a matter of minutes. I don't know how many people actually texted to donate, but I did hear that individual donations topped over $7 million in the first few days. And even more unexpectedly, my own Twitter account became a type of Ground Zero for information, where I could retweet information about missing persons, the nuclear crisis at the Fukushima reactor, and the grim casualty counts from outlying areas.

I was new to Twitter, so it came as a surprise that news outlets were following my tweets. CNN called that next day, asking for an interview. As the most prominent Japanese American actor and activist out there on the social media — not a hard spot to occupy, admittedly — it suddenly fell to me to spearhead the social media campaign. I followed up the Twitter work with a YouTube video, hastily assembled by my team of producers at my show *Allegiance* (who were kind enough to lend their logistical support — you'll hear a lot about them in this book, for without them I don't know how I'd have put much of my media together). The video took some of the most compelling pictures of the disaster, including amazing rescue and recovery efforts and examples of the selfless and stoic response of the Japanese people, and coupled them with another plea for assistance. Over 100,000 people watched that video within the first day of its release.

The disaster relief campaign taught me an early lesson in the power of social media, one that I have carried with me since. With just a few thousand fans, amplified by the power of Twitter, I was able to make a real difference in the lives of millions, as well as alert traditional media to our efforts. I soon thought to myself, "If I can make such an impact with just a few thousand fans, why not reach out and build a larger platform?" There was much work to be done, and causes near and dear to my heart that I wanted to speak out on. The question of same-sex marriage, for example, was reaching a critical crossroads. I also wanted to fulfill what I consider one of my life's missions: to ensure that the history and lessons of the Japanese American internment never be forgotten.

Fundamentally, I wanted to build a community that could laugh, share and discuss the pressing matters of society. Already on my Facebook page, fans were beginning to post very funny science- and science fiction-related images, called "memes" by the digerati. In the early days of my Facebook page, I would receive a dozen or so wall posts a day and sift through them, downloading the images I found particularly funny or inspiring. I never really knew at the time whether I would ever use them; I just enjoyed keeping them and laughing over them with Brad later (I've included many examples of these memes in this book, some of which I've had to revise or recreate because of a little thing called copyright).

But like my experience with the tsunami and Twitter, I soon found myself acting as a central gathering spot — a "node" if you will — for sharing some of the Internet's funniest memes. I say that knowing full well that I did not create any of these images; they were all sent to me by others. But there is real value in sharing — and real rewards. The number of fans on my Facebook page leapt from 25,000 to over 100,000 in a matter of days as word spread that Sulu had started a page and had "some pretty funny shit" on it, as many a fan wrote on my wall.

I must admit, at first I was quite taken aback by the number of shares and likes on each post, and I had to limit myself to just a few a day so as not to get too sucked in. It also took me months to understand what all the fuss and appeal was about. Fans had to explain it to me: Having Sulu as a Facebook "friend" was like "having a favorite gay uncle" — one with a somewhat naughty sense of humor.

"Okay, I get that," I said. And with that, my Internet career was born.

Twitter Sniping

When I first began sharing online, I spent a great deal of time on Twitter. I had no idea what I was doing, let alone whether anyone would want to read anything I tweeted. I hoped to say something that might rise above the fray, and do it in 140 characters or less. And I was delighted when fans responded, welcoming me to the Twitterverse. I even made sure each new follower received a thank you from me (eventually I had to discontinue this). I made a conscious decision, however, not to "follow" each fan who gave me a follow, as I knew it would quickly become impossible to read through my Twitter stream each day. I hoped fans would understand.

Truth be told, I wasn't even quite sure what Twitter

was for, or what good it would do anyone other than to read breaking news. But as the Tsunami relief efforts taught me, social media can be a powerful force for change. And so, with my daily tweet, I not only hoped to share funny advice or anecdotes, but to effect some kind of change.

One opportunity arose unexpectedly, when I suddenly found myself in a unique position to respond to the world's homophobes with my own brand of humor. Victoria Jackson, a comedienne who had a stint on *Saturday Night Live* many years ago, was the first I felt compelled to answer. She had gone on a very public rant about how the show *Glee* was supposedly turning boys gay, presumably because it is filled with musical theater moments. At first, I thought she must be joking or had lost her marbles. Anyone these days knows that you don't "turn" someone gay, nor can you "convert" them through "therapy", bringing them squealing back from the Great Pink Path. Indeed, I'm pleased that a recent California law expressly rejects and outlaws such practices. Even more ludicrous is the idea that a few song and dance numbers on a FOX television show might spread The Gay. But Ms. Jackson continued her shrill tirade, and so out of "exasperation," I tweeted this:

Former SNL star Victoria Jackson thinks
Glee is turning boys gay. I think Victoria
Jackson is more to blame for that.

about 1 hour ago via Twitterfeed
Retweeted by 100+ people   ↰ Reply ⇄ Retweet

 GeorgeTakei
George Takei

Now, normally I don't care to make fun of someone's physical appearance unless it's my husband's
(he once was a svelte marathon runner; now I just
tell him there's more of him to love). But you must
admit, Ms. Jackson was asking for this kind of response. If she really believes exposure to some ex-
ternal influence can turn young boys gay, surely the
sight of her in all her present corpulence would have
a greater gay-ifying effect.

The "comedian" Tracy Morgan was another real
piece of work. He is filled with such hatred toward
LGBT people that, during one routine, he actually
declared that he would kill his own son if he found
out he were gay. I was shocked to hear such a horri-
fying threat, particularly from someone in the entertainment field who works daily with gay people and
LGBT allies such as the remarkable Tina Fey, who
— to her great credit — took Morgan to task for his
outburst. This time news outlets began contacting me
for a response. My tweet followed quickly after:

In a stand-up rant, Tracy Morgan threatened to kill his son if he were gay. I suspect his dad is next for naming him Tracy.

about 10 minutes ago via Hootsuite
Retweeted by 1000+ people

Reply Retweet

 GeorgeTakei
George Takei

Now, I didn't know at the time that Tracy's father was already dead, or I would have tempered that a bit. That was an "oops." But my objective was to answer hatred with humor, to "defang the snake," as it were. I could spend hours arguing about how violence, or even the threat of violence against LGBT people is a societal plague. I could expound at length on how bullying and homophobia account for up to one-third of all teen suicides. I could ask someone like Tracy directly if he condones violence against minorities, or how he would feel if someone threatened to kill his son if he were born black, as I presume he would be. But that's really someone else's job. My own feeling is that laughter, irony, and ridicule are the best responses to this type of behavior. Giving someone like Tracy any more stage time for his weird, sad rant would solve nothing.

Another person for whom I share little love is former Governor of California, Arnold Schwarzenegger. This movie actor-cum-politician ran on a platform of liberal social policy and fiscal conservatism, and I believed in my heart that he would stand by his principles on the question of same-sex marriage. After many years, the California Legislature finally passed a marriage bill that would allow my then-partner of nearly 20 years Brad and me to be married and enjoy the same rights and privileges afforded to heterosexual couples in the Golden State. I thought to myself, "This is going to happen. The Governor said he supports equality, and we are finally going to have it."

Imagine my surprise and indignation when The Governator instead vetoed the legislation, saying, among other things, that this was a matter for the courts to decide, not our elected representatives. Of course, when courts overturn same-sex marriage bans, you'll hear the same people complaining the courts are legislating from the bench; they'll simply blame whichever branch of government sides with LGBT rights at the time. Schwarzenegger's act of vetoing the bill was the heat that finally got me steamed enough to take action. I'm speaking specifically about the step of coming out publicly to the press. I had been "out" for some time among family and friends, but had never taken the public step of alerting the press. And as an actor, you're not really out until you're out to the press, believe me.

As the world now knows, for Arnold Schwarzenegger to take any position with respect to family values, marriage or morality is truly the height of irony. So when his own scandal broke, I saw no reason to hold back. I tweeted this, with a geeky Sci-fi reference thrown in for good measure:

> **Schwarzenegger confesses to fathering baby with house staff member, but explains that child is destined to bring down SkyNet in 2031**
>
> about 30 minutes ago via Hootsuite
> Retweeted by 1500+ people   ↩ Reply ⇄ Retweet

 GeorgeTakei
George Takei

This turned out to be one of my most popular tweets. But I only learned this after the Webmaster for *Allegiance* pointed me to a site that actually tracks Twitter virality. I had no idea anyone even cared enough to monitor such things.

Another popular tweet played upon the hypocrisy of some of the rants of the Fundamentalists. They frequently cite The Old Testament as proof not only that God is on their side, but that He really doesn't like gay people. The truth is, you can find almost anything in the Bible to latch onto if you are really determined. The prohibitions in the Old Testament are not only archaic, but wide reaching. So, after hearing yet another righteous citation to restrictions thousands of years past their usefulness, I tweeted this:

> **Tomorrow I'm going to violate Leviticus by wearing a cotton/polyester blend. #CherryPickingSins**
>
> about 2 hours ago via Hootsuite
> Retweeted by 1500+ people   ↰ Reply ⇄ Retweet

 GeorgeTakei
George Takei

It wasn't really true. I don't care for polyester. But the tweet resonated, I believe, not only because it pointed out an obvious double standard, but also because there's something funny about imagining a senior citizen violating Leviticus.

We don't have that many elderly spokespersons of comedy these days. We once had the great George Burns, and Bob Hope, and Johnny Carson. Today, of course, we have Betty White, who recently turned 90. I've learned that when you get to be a certain age, you can get away with saying a lot of things, some of which wouldn't even be remotely funny if someone forty years younger said them. *The Golden Girls* ran for years off the same theory and basically used the same four jokes for seven marvelous seasons. I've recently suggested that Betty and I should do a TV series about two seniors living together in an unlikely pairing of a widow and a naughty gay best buddy. We could call it *Friends with Government Benefits*.

In my tweets, I also try to stay current, not only with news, but with pop culture. I read the Hollywood press, and I see every film up for an Academy Award for Best Picture (this is actually my responsibility, as I'm a voting member of the Academy). I don't generally listen to rock music. But when I do, I believe some classics should remain undisturbed.

Miley Cyrus records cover of "Smells Like Teen Spirit." Kobain fans now understand his early departure.

about 2 hours ago via Hootsuite
Retweeted by 1000+ people   ↩ Reply ↻ Retweet

 GeorgeTakei
George Takei

It's hard to believe, but Kurt Cobain died more than 18 years ago, back in 1994. Miley Cyrus was only 1½ years old when he passed. For some reason, while the 1990s seemed to be a huge decade of change and progress, the years after 2000 all blend together.

I still think 1990 was 10 years ago

Here's another thing about tweets: You never know if something is going to get "retweeted" much, which is problematic because retweets are what draw fans to my account. Unlike more prolific tweeters, I tried to limit my tweets to one a day and to make them count. For a time, I actually made the effort to track how well they were received, if only to gauge whether they had any resonance with my followers. A pattern soon emerged. A tweet would receive high traction if it was among the first commentaries on breaking news. That traction would be increased greatly if it were funny, particularly if it made a pop cultural reference that had to be inferred. This latter point was important: I wanted to build a following of engaged thinkers, not merely fans. I had no need or patience for those who cared only about my work on TV or film. For me, social media needed to be an interactive, not reactive, endeavor. And a retweet had to say implicitly, "I get this joke and approve."

Once a tweet enters the Twitterstream, however, there's no real way to build much of any discussion around it. Sure, there are hashtags to provide a mechanism to enable me to go back and read what others had tweeted on the same topic, but I found the whole thing rather cumbersome. It admittedly took me a while even to figure out what the hashtag "#FF @georgetakei" meant. Where my mind first went with that isn't fit for print; let's just say I thought it was pronounced "Pound-F-F George Takei."

A tweet also lives on forever once it's out, even if you delete it from your homepage. And there are some tweets that I've come to regret, even if they were funny at the time. For example, when Donald Trump was running for President, I was rather unimpressed with his "birther" campaign against Obama. It seemed to drag us into a non-issue over and over again.

So when his campaign finally ran out of steam, I was both relieved and amused, tweeting this:

Donald Trump bows out of presidential race, citing inability to prove he wasn't born a douchebag.

about 10 minutes ago via Hootsuite
Retweeted by 1000+ people

⤺ Reply ⇄ Retweet

GeorgeTakei
George Takei

I've had the pleasure of meeting Mr. Trump personally and even going on his show, *Celebrity Apprentice*, on which I only lasted three weeks. I'm told that my "exit" from the show was gracious, which I'm relieved to hear since it was an extremely frustrating loss that did not seem deserved at the time. While Mr. Trump and I disagree on many matters, including the question of marriage equality, I found him quite willing to listen to the other side. I've even invited him to sit down with me over lunch at Jean-Georges in Trump International Hotel Central Park to hear me out on the question, an invitation he's accepted in principle, but we haven't yet had the opportunity to make happen. So I wouldn't describe him as a "douchebag" today, even after his awkward "October '12 Surprise" that fizzled like the career of an *American Idol* winner. This goes to show even my mind can be changed after seven and a half decades of living.

Some of the better times I spent on Twitter involved

37

following the occasional Twitter feud (or in the case of the dispute between fans of *Star Wars* and *Star Trek*, the occasional Twitter peace — more on that later). I even had my own friendly feud with the comedian Gilbert Gottfried, whose name I always seem to misspell. Gottfreed roasted me at the Friars Club and I've worked with him on films before, including voicing Disney animations together, so let me first assure readers that we are on friendly terms. That didn't stop Gottfreid from launching into me one fateful week.

It was shortly after the Japanese Tsunami in 2011, and Gotfreid had just been summarily fired from his job voicing the Aflac duck on account of his tasteless humor aimed at victims of the disaster. As one of the international spokesmen for disaster relief, and as a member of the Twitterati with a growing and active following, I was a natural target for Gilbert's ribbing, particularly after I tagged him in a post but once again misspelled his name. He began posting things from his highly active Twitter account hoping to get my attention. Here is a quick sample of some of his tweets:

"@GeorgeTakei Hey #Queer, learn to spell my name."

When I demurred, he upped the ante:

38

"Tracy Morgan is in trouble with the gays, me with the Japanese. Whatever you do, don't make any jokes about @GeorgeTakei!!!"

"@GeorgeTakei Hey George, I heard when Star Trek was on, the pay was really low, but you received a lot in the back-end."

I tried to deflect the attack, tweeting that unfortunately I don't speak Chihuahua. But that only seemed to inflame him further:

"Hey @Georgetakei, That comment was hard to swallow. But I guess you've never had that problem."

My followers started to point out on chat boards that Godtfreid was gunning for me, and try as I might to ignore the barrage, his Twitter guns kept firing. Then came this tweet:

@GeorgeTakei follows me! I don't mean on Twitter. I mean into the Men's Room where he blows me!!!

about 2 hourse ago via web
Retweeted by 20 people

☆
↰
Reply ↻ Retweet

RealGilbert
Gilbert Gottfried

Le sigh. I realized that "shields" were not enough to dissuade Godfreet; I needed to bring out my own Twitter torpedoes:

@RealGilbert **Friend, the only thing that's been blown lately is your career. #DuckAndCover**

about 20 minutes ago via Twitterfeed
Retweeted by 2000+ people

⤴ Reply ⟲ Retweet

GeorgeTakei
George Takei

For this exchange, and others, Buzzfeed unexpectedly awarded me with the best Twitter stream of 2011, the above exchange being their #1 pick. Oh my, my, my. But for me, the real future of social media clearly wasn't in a top-down, mostly text-based world of truncated messaging. Twitter was great for receiving instant news, posting quick updates and links, and growing a basic following. But answering fans became far too demanding, and going through my "interactions" and "mentions" on a daily basis was proving too much of a time sink.

And so, perhaps to the dismay of my avid Twitter followers, I backed off. By October of 2011, I had begun to focus on my Facebook page and was gaining much broader traction, and the ability to share images and talk about them collectively as a community was simply too enticing. My heavy Twitter days were more or less done — you might even say my Twitter campaign was in full retweet.

Waka Waka Into Mordor

ONE DOES NOT SIMPLY WAKA WAKA INTO MORDOR

--FOZZY BEAR

During my first few months of Facebooking, I discovered that my page had fostered a collective nostalgia for specific cultural icons. These started, unsurprisingly, within the realm of science fiction and fantasy. They commonly included a pointy-eared Vulcan from a certain groundbreaking 1960s television show.

Just as often, though, I found myself sharing images of a diminutive, ancient, green and disarmingly wise Jedi Master who speaks in flip-side down English.

Or, if feeling more sinister, I'd post pictures of his black-cloaked, dark-sided, heavy-breathing nemesis. As an aside, I initially received from *Star Trek* fans considerable "push-back," or at least many raised Spock brows, when I began sharing images of Yoda and Darth Vader. To the purists, this bordered on sacrilege.. But as I like to remind fans, I was the only actor to work within both franchises, having also voiced the part of Lok Durd from the animated show *Star Wars: The Clone Wars.*

It was the virality of these early posts, shared by thousands of fans without any prodding from me, that got me thinking. Why *do* we love Spock, Yoda and Darth Vader so much? And what is it about characters like these that causes fans to click "like" and "share" so readily?

One thing was clear: Cultural icons help people define who they are today because they shaped who they were as children. We all "like" Yoda because we all loved *The Empire Strikes Back*, probably watched it many times, and can recite our favorite lines. Indeed, we all can quote Yoda, and we all have tried out our best impression of him.

When someone posts a meme of Yoda, many immediately share it, not just because they think it is funny (though it usually is — it's hard to go wrong with the Master), but because it says something about the sharer. It's shorthand for saying, "This little guy made a huge impact on me, not sure what it is, but for certain a huge impact. Did it make one on you, too? I'm clicking 'share' to affirm something you may not know about me. I 'like' Yoda."

And isn't that what sharing on Facebook is all about? It's not simply that the sharer wants you to snortle or "LOL" as it were. That's part of it, but not the core. *At* its core is a statement about one's belief system, one that includes the wisdom of Yoda.

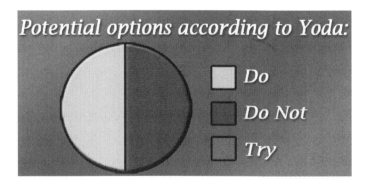

Other eminently shareable icons included beloved Tolkien characters, particularly Gandalf (as played by the inimitable Sir Ian McKellan). Gandalf, like Yoda, is somehow always above reproach and unfailingly epic.

© *Leticia Wilson, leremy - Fotolia.com. Used with Permission*

Like Yoda, Gandalf has his darker counterpart. Gollum is a fan favorite because he is a fallen figure who could reform with the right guidance. It doesn't hurt that his every meme is invariably read in his distinctive, blood-curdling rasp. I recall with fondness one popular meme:

Then there's also Batman, who seems to have survived both Adam West and Christian Bale, but whose questionable relationship to the Boy Wonder left plenty of room for hilarious homoerotic undertones. But seriously, there is something about the brooding, misunderstood and "chaotic-good" nature of this superhero that touches all of our hearts.

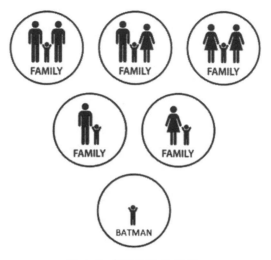

Photo Credit © Keith G. Richie.
Used with Permission

Although my "most-shared" posts began with sci-fi and fantasy, I found that fans universally longed for other things. For some reason, the Muppets — the classic, ragtag set of misbegotten optimists — also made their way commonly into pics shared on my wall. Perhaps it's the simple wonder of a non-traditional, cross-species marriage between a frog and a pig that never fails to provoke a smile. I was particularly delighted to see Jim Henson's estate pull its advertisements with "Chick-fil-A" after that company's CEO and management came out strongly against same-sex marriage. Often when I'm stuck wondering about what I should post, I come back to these furred, fluffed, and fisted fellows. The latter adjective reminds me of a cartoon, which I can't reprint here, depicting Kermit about to receive his X-ray results. The X-ray shows a skeletal arm deep inside Kermit's innards, the doctor saying, "What I'm about to tell you may come as a shock…"

For my fans born in the 1960s, Spock, Kermit, and Batman were icons of their early childhood that, to the delight of us all, maintain continued cultural relevance today. Indeed, *Star Trek* movies still roll out to entertain and inspire whole new audiences, even if the cast comprises a whole set of new, fresh faces. Kermit and Miss Piggy have made a comeback, moving back into their original stage in Hollywood. And meanwhile, after many franchises, The Dark Knight still rises in theaters.

I cannot mention the last fact without feeling profound sadness and loss for those killed by a lone, deranged gunman in Colorado while gathered for the midnight premiere showing of that film. I was so struck by the senselessness of it that I was compelled to put out a simple message that day:

> *MANY VICTIMS OF TODAY'S TRAGEDY WERE FANS OF SCIENCE FICTION/FANTASY. THEY STOOD IN LINE TO BE THE FIRST TO SEE, TO BE INSPIRED, AND TO ESCAPE. AS A COMMUNITY OF DREAMERS, WE MOURN THIS TERRIBLE TRAGEDY AND THIS SENSELESS TAKING OF INNOCENT LIVES.*
>
> *--GEORGE TAKEI*

Beyond well-known characters, like the Muppets or Batman, many fans share a love for other lost symbols of an "America-that-once-was." These fans were children when cassette tapes were wound by No. 2 pencils, when "film" was held in black plastic cases resembling Tupperware, and when young artists drew cityscapes using control knobs on a red television-like screen filled with magnetic powder. They grew up knowing what this meant when you came into the classroom in the morning:

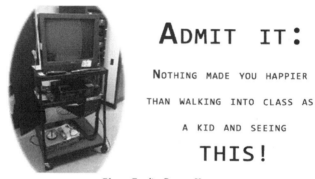

ADMIT IT:

NOTHING MADE YOU HAPPIER

THAN WALKING INTO CLASS AS

A KID AND SEEING

THIS!

Photo Credit: Steven Karns.
Used with Permission.

In fairness, when I was growing up, we didn't even have VCRs or Movie Day at school, but Generation X and the Baby Boomers did. I am mindful of the generational divide, and I sometimes even test it — as when I post lyrics side by side from today versus the 1970s:

"Stairway to Heaven" vs. 1971	"Stupid Ho" 2012
There's a lady who's sure	You a stupid ho
all that glitters is gold	You a stupid ho
And she's buying a	You a stupid ho
stairway to heaven.	You a stupid ho
See a difference?	

Young people are quick to jump to the defense of the music of these times, but a part of me wonders whether music has somehow peaked. Listening to Lady Gaga today, it sounds an awful lot like Madge in the 1990s. Boy bands are pretty much still boy bands. The only new developments seem to be the incorporation of rap moments in otherwise melodic pop tunes and the prevalence of auto-tune, neither of which appear to have advanced the art form appreciably.

But I digress. My Facebook page has become a sort of cultural barometer that I find truly fascinating. Nothing much happens by the way of pop culture without at least some fan posting about it on my wall. So even at the age of 75, I feel more or less current in today's goings-on. Some may find it surprising that my fan base, according to the statistics posted on Facebook, is not made up of mostly aging Trekkies over the age of 50. To the contrary, the largest demographic on my page is males between the age of 25 and 34 (what I call the Comedy Central crowd — they love anything I post about *South Park* or *Family Guy*), followed closely by females in the same age bracket. I'm not exactly sure when this shift occurred, but it delights me to know that, though I am separated in age by some forty or fifty years from most of my fans, they have welcomed me into their lives. As my fan base tilts ever younger, fewer and fewer fans will know me merely as "that guy who played Sulu."

Perhaps my page carries some favor because I often explore the common cultural ground beneath us. Take, for instance, the world's nearly unanimous love for Harry Potter. The Baby Boomers, now mostly in their 60s, are beginning to read these stories aloud to their grandchildren. At the same time, young people are quick to embrace it as their own epic saga. Who among us hasn't dreamed of waking up to find that we are destined for more than mere Mugglehood? The children in these stories awaken universal desires in us: the quest for greatness, the pull of companionship and love, a sense of clarity in our moral choices, an abiding belief in the magical and wondrous, and the ability to talk to snakes.

Compare *that* to the banal, static and self-absorbed story that is *Twilight*. Now, it's no secret that I am not a lover of this series. I made this clear in my call for the Star Alliance, which I'll cover in my next chapter. You see, cultural icons stand the test of time because they speak to our deeper convictions and ignite our dreams. There is more story in a minor character like Boba Fett than there is in all the clutter of various vampires in the *Twilight* franchise.

If it is our collective adoration for these characters that brings us together, then I am more than happy to be the purveyor of such images on a daily basis. Like holiday carols, Rubik's cubes, and reruns of *The Brady Bunch*, they remind us all that we were shaped by common cultural experiences that carried with them a common guiding set of values. While critics often wring their hands over the presumed superficiality of these icons and values, particularly given the poverty and afflictions of most of the rest of the world, they fail to offer up a workable alternative. If leadership requires a fired-up sense of purpose and imagination, it also demands a profound connection to the society to be led. Like it or not, this is our culture, and we should embrace and celebrate it, even while we strive to refine and shape it.

Meanwhile, I'm going to go watch some *Muppet Show* reruns and work on my best Yoda.

The Star Alliance

About a year ago, I received a tweet from a fan informing me that the *Chicago Sun Times* film critic, Roger Ebert, had called upon me to broker a peace. It was intriguing, to say the least. Mr. Ebert had been following a growing online feud between two of sci-fi's heavyweights — Carrie Fisher and William Shatner (no pun intended, Bill).

Bill had begun the spat by ridiculing the *Star Wars* franchise during an interview. He claimed that *Star Wars* was less original than *Star Trek*, and that *Trek* had a leg up over *Wars* when it came to character development and story line. "*Star Trek* had relationships and conflict among the relationships, and stories that involved humanity and philosophical questions. *Star*

Wars was special effects," he stated. "*Star Wars* was derivative of us by - what, 10, 15, 20 years?" He then took the character of Princess Leia on directly: "As beautiful as she was, and as wonderful an actress as she is, (she) can't compare to the marvelous heroines we had on *Star Trek*."

Now, Bill likes to stir the pot, particularly if he has a new show coming out, and he does not do things without knowing the consequences. You can't fire a photon torpedo across the bow of an Imperial Destroyer without some kind of response. It wasn't long before Carrie Fisher hit back with her own interview, "*Star Wars* was sooooooo much better than *Star Trek*," she said. She compared Klingon to a laundry detergent (I confess, I chuckled when I heard this), and noted that the original series appeared to lack any kind of budget for special effects. To add some personal insult to injury, she mocked Bill's weight gain since retiring as Captain of the *Enterprise*, then cheekily added that her own "space buns" were superior to Spock's ears.

Abe Gurko   Carrie Fisher

The Shat then fired back, in yet another video, claiming he could in fact still fit in his uniform with a bit of pushing on the stretch material, but that he doubted Fisher could still fit into her bikini worn in the third movie. Yes, it had turned quite personal.

Of course, it was all in good fun, but beneath it all a nagging question remained: Was Bill correct that *Star Wars'* use of special effects detracted from the story and characters? Was Ms. Fisher far off the mark in criticizing the admittedly shaky effects of the original series?

It didn't take long for the Internet to grow abuzz, with sci-fi fans rushing to the defense of their favored "Star" series. While *Star Trek* had lasted through the ages, *Star Wars* concededly had gained far greater pop culture penetration. Geeks everywhere were taking sides, and a rupture in the sci-fi continuum seemed possible. So when Roger Ebert's blog covered the feud, he wondered aloud whether a peace could be made between the two warring sides: "One can only hope George Takei (*Star Trek*'s Lt. Sulu) can be brought in to broker a peace settlement before blood is shed."

I'm not exactly sure why Ebert chose to ask for my assistance. Did he know that I had worked on *Star Wars* as well as *Star Trek* and thus stood in some unique position? Did he pick me because I had already successfully begun an online presence, and had a few viral videos under my belt? Or was there something authoritative about my delivery that he believed could quiet the growing storm?

I jest of course. I happily accepted the challenge, and I did not take this assignment lightly. I told them both to shut their wormholes, before images like this began to appear:

Indeed, a fracture between the two fan bases of the two titans of science fiction threatened to pull our collective attentions away at a time when focus, unity and singularity of purpose was much needed.

I was speaking, of course, about the common threat that was *Twilight*.

In my video calling for the Star Alliance against *Twilight*, I went into some of the basic reasons why that movie series (I confess, I have not read the books — and if they are anything like the film, I don't care to) could poison an entire generation's mindset toward science fiction. For me, both *Star Trek* and *Star Wars* represent the expansion of human imagination, creativity, and curiosity. In the best of science fiction, epic battles rage between forces of good and evil, and the fate of the universe often hangs in the balance. Noble and stirring characters inhabit the big screen, challenging us to be heroes, to rise to our fullest potential, and to vanquish our enemies utterly. Great lessons are taught to, and absorbed by, young minds and hearts.

In *Twilight*, not so. Unlike the great vampires of the Anne Rice series, *The Lost Boys* movie or, more recently, *True Blood*, there is nothing "bad ass" in the least about the *Twilight* bloodsuckers. In that simpering world, centuries-old vampires mope over 17-year olds, attend high school, and sparkle in the sunlight.

The main, driving question throughout the first of the three films was not a struggle for domination, a gripping test of the limits of camaraderie, or even a quest for something long since thought unattainable. No, *Twilight* asked the same burning question so many *Tiger Beat* features demand of their readers: "Does my boyfriend like me?"

Okay, okay. We had a great deal of fun at the expense of poor *Twilight*, and fan memes dutifully flooded my page. My favorites depicted various vampire hunters — Buffy, Blade, Abraham Lincoln — in hot pursuit of sparkly, pale Edward. Other fans chimed in with humor about the banality of the books:

Once Upon a Time...

I fell asleep on my human's keyboard, and I accidentally wrote the next Twilight.

All manner of images surfaced suggesting that Darth Vader and Stormtroopers, even in their helmets, had greater diversity in their expressions than a hapless, poorly-directed Kristen Stewart.

I shared these with the fans in good humor, and unsurprisingly the supporters of *Twilight* cried foul. "Stop bashing *Twilight*, I love that film!" "Just because YOU don't understand *Twilight* doesn't mean others can't love it." "Edward is sooooo dreamy!!" To me, their defense of the franchise often lacked conviction. The "Twihards" knew, deep down, that what they were enjoying in these films was a guilty pleasure, and not great storytelling, profound character development or even groundbreaking special effects.

Moreover, what kind of message was *Twilight* sending to girls and young women everywhere? Compare the noteworthy heroines of other books and series: Hermione Granger, who through study and dedication helped her friends vanquish the greatest of Dark Wizards; Arya Stark, who vows to avenge her family and learns to fence with the greatest of Dancing Masters; Katniss Everdeen, who replaces her doomed sister in a battle to the death and, through her defiance, sparks a revolution against the Capitol. As an aside, one of my favorite fan-shared memes related to her:

© *pink candy - Fotolia.com - Used with permission.*

The Alliance was a turning point for my Facebook page. As broker of the Star Peace, I was granted not just grudging but enthusiastic permission to post all things science fiction. Die-hard sci-fi fans clamored for an expansion of the Star Alliance, to include such great series as *Battlestar Galactica*, *Babylon 5*, *Dr. Who*, and *Stargate*. For a brief time I even sold T-shirts for the Alliance (all proceeds benefiting the non-profit Old Globe Theater's production of my show *Allegiance*). Fans came up with brilliant logos that used the space vessels of various shows to spell the word "COEXIST" just as religious symbols had been used in versions past to form that same hopeful word.

Science fiction is more than just our collective

dreams for a human race that reaches to the stars. In many ways, the dreams of yesterday are becoming the realities of today and the path for tomorrow. It amazes me these days to see so many of the concepts first imagined on *Star Trek* gaining practical application. Our communicators look very much like the early cellular flip-phones. Scientists propose rocket engines powered by, believe it or not, dilithium crystals. Even the concept of warp drive has moved into mainstream theory. Perhaps Gene Roddenberry was a modern-day Leonardo da Vinci, so many of his imaginings coming to pass.

So is it time for yet another great Star series to come along and lift our eyes and spirits to the heavens? I would hope so, and I can't wait.

Oh Myyy!

<u>Bacon</u>

We've all seen it. People love to post pictures of their pricey restaurant meals or fancy entrées they've managed to prepare themselves for that special some-one. As supportive Facebook friends, we dutifully click "like" to show our appreciation for the beauty of the presentation and the imagined delicacy of the flavors. We do this even though we know the post was simply offered to render us resentful, envious, and hungry.

But when it comes to food posts, there's no beating America's favorite bad boy edible: Bacon.

Fans "share" and "like" posts about bacon with the gusto of studio audiences applauding Emeril Lagasse's extra bulb of garlic, tossed into the pot with a "Bam!" Behind it churns the same primal instinct that causes us to nod with approval at things like fried Twinkies (an endangered species after the recent bankruptcy of Hostess Foods), Krispy Kreme donuts, or a whole stick of butter in Paula Dean's Southern Casseroles. Incidentally, there was a period when deep fried turkeys, an invention of the South, were all the rage for Thanksgiving. But because so many of those who attempted this were badly burned, it has largely petered out as a fad. If you really need to do this, make sure you set it up outside, in a very large pot, and with a portable burner. There was also a time where Turduckens — a combination of a turkey, stuffed with a duck, stuffed with a chicken — were on everyone's Thanksgiving try list. One of my favorite cartoons showed each of these three birds in the same bed, the turkey smoking a cigarette, a simple caption reading: "And they would never speak of the Turducken again."

But back to bacon. As I understand it, "liking" a bacon post is culinary and nutritional defiance. It ignores decades of scientific study on arteriosclerosis and the carcinogenic nature of processed foods. We know bacon is chock-full of sodium, fat, nitrates and more fat. In glorifying bacon, we reclaim a simpler time when we could eat what we wanted to, as we did as children once upon a time, before restaurants began publishing caloric values of food, and packaging cautioned us about fat percentages in our food. When we eat bacon, we throw caution to the wind and truly *live*, if even just a little.

I'd be remiss if I didn't also mention that "bacon" also has been the unintended beneficiary of the low-level pop static of a certain "Kevin," the namesake of one of the best parlor games ever invented.

I've sometimes imagined that if sin had a flavor, it might very well be bacon. It even tastes smoky, as if it emerged piping hot out of the fiery pans of hell. More than any forbidden fruit, this delectable treat — best when crispy, the little grease bubbles still dancing happily on its crenelated edges — epitomizes things we know we shouldn't eat, but still crave and keep going back to. In short, it's food crack.

Photo Credit: store.thebaconshop.com
Used with Permission

Most fans (mostly men) who left comments on this highly popular post swore they'd take bacon roses over normal roses any day. I suppose this supports the old adage that a way to a man's heart is through his stomach. It's no coincidence then that Homer Simpson has become the unofficial champion of bacon.

Fans of bacon tend to see it in all manner of places, especially in street signs. Everywhere they turn, the world reminds them that they could be somewhere else. Somewhere with bacon.

I can never look at wavy side-by-side lines on a road sign the same way again. Here's another:

Perhaps it's the naughty aspect of bacon that makes it so appealing. Bacon images wouldn't be nearly as popular if bacon were something we got to see or eat every day without judgment. It's like boobs in Europe. They're all over their beaches, so it's just not that big a deal. But like Big Mac Lasagnas (yes, that's right, Big Mac Lasagnas. Google it), bacon is just too bad for you to pass up.

Fast food chains have started taking this to extremes. Burger King introduced a "bacon sundae" — combining two things we know are terrible for us into a single, unforgivable treat. Even high-end restaurants have begun offering bacon as part of their fancier offerings, sometimes slipping it into desserts. I once witnessed, as a particularly tempting selection, a dish of maple ice cream over corn bread, with chopped center-cut smokehouse bacon, all smothered in rich syrup. My stomach rumbles at the memory.

The overly health-conscious among us have tried to rain on the bacon parade by promoting low fat (and low flavor) options, such as turkey bacon. Turkey bacon. It's like saying "shoot" instead of "shit." It just doesn't quite carry the moment.

I've noticed that bacon substitute is typically paired with another disappointing partner, like egg whites, and served with a side of arugula salad, instead of the buttered home fries wedges you'd rather have. Brad stays on my case to eat healthy, and I do make the effort. However, there's a part of my brain — the part wrapped in bacon — that protests. Life is too short to not order the bacon dessert. As a matter of fact, life starts to feel mighty long when all you eat is turkey bacon and egg whites and a side of arugula.

That's Not Funny

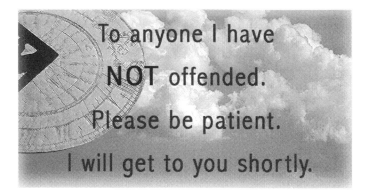

To anyone I have NOT offended. Please be patient. I will get to you shortly.

I quickly learned that, on the Internet, it is impossible to please everyone, but really easy to piss them all off. A joke that I find chuckle-worthy, an inevitable percentage of viewers will find in poor, or even wretched, taste. And of course, it is those folks who will take the time to let me know exactly why, usually in a wrenching, over-personal comment or email:

"GEORGE, YOU'RE SUCH A CHAMPION OF HUMAN RIGHTS, AND OF THE VOICELESS AND DOWNTRODDEN. WHY WOULD YOU MAKE FUN OF OLD PEOPLE WHO RIDE AROUND IN LARKS? I'M A DIFFERENT-LY-ABLED PERSON IN A WHEELCHAIR, A STATUS I'VE HAD MOST OF MY ADULT LIFE AFTER A TERRIBLE, LIFE-CHANGING ACCIDENT. YOUR POST HURT ME, AND I'M STILL CRYING AS I WRITE THIS. ISN'T WHAT YOU POSTED JUST ANOTHER FORM OF BULLYING?!?"

Good grief. If we can't laugh at ourselves, and at one another, in good spirit and without malice, then what fun can be left? If we must withhold all ribbing in the name of protecting everyone's feelings, then we truly are a toothless society. We will reach what I call "the lowest common denominator of butthurt."

More recently, during the launch of the iPhone 5, I posted something a fan had sent me that I found wickedly satirical. It showed a police officer asking a homeless man to go camp in front of the Apple store like everyone else. Within minutes, I was accused by many fans of making a joke "at the expense" of the homeless. Dozens voiced their indignation over my "poor taste." And more than a few fans expressed their sheer outrage at the blatant use of Comic Sans in the caption.

But seriously. Have we as a society forgotten the important place of satire in our cultural dialogue? Have we grown so afraid of offending that we no longer dare pose the hard questions, or even the easy ones? Anyone who missed the irony of our government (represented by the police officer) asking those without money (the homeless chap) to go and camp beside those with money to spend on iPhones either wasn't paying much attention, or needs a refresher course in political humor. And anyone who thought I was condemning the homeless rather than the state of our society clearly doesn't know me very well.

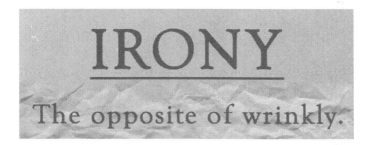

IRONY

The opposite of wrinkly.

When words and images become too politically volatile to even speak or print, we have lost something indeed. I discovered this early on in my Internet forays. When I filmed my "douchebag" video, I called out Arkansas school board member, Clint McCance, for posting on Facebook that he enjoyed it when gays "give each other AIDS and die." What a role model for our children. McCance apologized clumsily for his "hasty" words, but not before embarrassing himself, his school district, and probably the entire state of Arkansas.

I was determined to answer back with something that would cut to the quick. But I could think of no way to describe Mr. McCance other than as a "douchebag." Brad worried at the time that "douche-bag" was too vulgar for me to say, at least outside the set of *The Howard Stern Show* (nothing is too vulgar once inside that set). Although Brad finally relented and let me say it — ultimately to over a million viewers on YouTube, goodness me — neither of us expected the torrent of reproach that I would receive.

Apparently, calling someone a "douchebag" is an offense to all women, at least according to the feminine hygiene police. I've never understood the logic to this. A receptacle for douche liquid is certainly not a very nice thing to be called. But neither is "Santorum," and the gay community isn't getting its panties in a bunch over it. Perhaps that's because we learned long ago to laugh at ourselves.

The fact is, the "douche" is an invention, by men, that tells women they need to wash out their vaginas to be truly clean — in other words, a totally unnecessary and demeaning contraption. Logically, calling someone this would be no slight upon women at all.

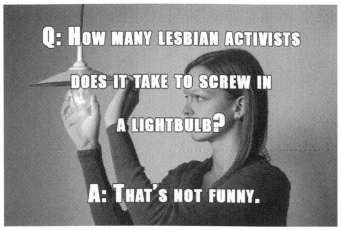

© Bernd Jürgens - Fotolia.com
Used with Permission.

Let's just agree that "douchebag" has nothing to do with women or their bodily functions.

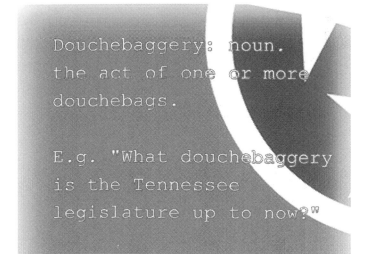

73

In fact, no one even thinks of girly parts at all when you call someone a douchebag. They might, however, think of Clint McCance.

Another common objection concerns name-calling itself. According to the Sensitive Sallies of the world, the use of pejoratives against those who bully and oppress is to be condemned itself as bullying. I once reposted something Morgan Freeman tweeted:

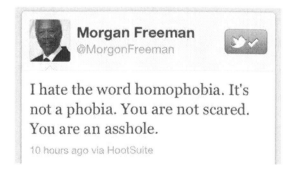

Morgan Freeman
@MorgonFreeman

I hate the word homophobia. It's not a phobia. You are not scared. You are an asshole.

10 hours ago via HootSuite

Within minutes of the post, the name-calling police were on the scene with acceptability filters armed and ready, reminding me (as if I needed it) that calling people "assholes" because, well, they are acting like assholes, isn't going to accomplish anything or change any minds.

I beg to differ. Nobody likes to be thought of as an asshole, any more than anyone likes being thought of as a douche or a monster or a dickwad. So pointing out that people who think of themselves as homophobes are in fact acting like assholes has a decent shot of having some effect.

More importantly, the tweet was funny. Come on, it's funny. It's surprising, concise and dead-on true. That's why it resonates, and why so many people shared it, including me. It said what so many have wanted to say but never quite had the right vocabulary to articulate. As with the douchebags of the world, calling an asshole an asshole sometimes is exactly what needs to happen.

Indeed, it's even funnier that Morgan Freeman tweeted it, because you can't help but hear it in his voice.

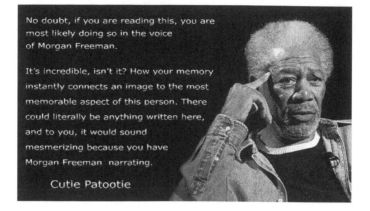

No doubt, if you are reading this, you are most likely doing so in the voice of Morgan Freeman.

It's incredible, isn't it? How your memory instantly connects an image to the most memorable aspect of this person. There could literally be anything written here, and to you, it would sound mesmerizing because you have Morgan Freeman narrating.

Cutie Patootie

When it comes to the proper place of humor, I do have one caveat. There is a time for us to laugh together, and a time when it simply is just "too soon." Jon Stewart famously delayed further airings of *The Daily Show* for over a week after the events of 9/11. And my friend Gilbert Gotfread really ought to have delayed, perhaps permanently, his barrage of tsunami and dead Japanese jokes that came on the heels of that terrible tragedy.

Even science fiction fans have reminded me that some wounds are simply too fresh, as with my re-post of what Alderaan looks like now, which elicited many condemnations of "too soon."

In other news, on Alderaan...

As the old saying goes, I was simply looking for fan love, in Alderaan places.

The notion that something is "too soon" has bitten me in the proverbial ass before. For example, a fan sent me a picture of a capsized cruise liner with a smiling "Isaac the Bartender" giving the thumbs up. Not knowing that rescue operations had failed to recover certain passengers, I reposted the picture. I learned with dismay — minutes later from many fans — that families were still in shock and grief over their missing loved ones. I was mortified. I immediately took down the post and issued an apology for the ill-conceived share. This is one of the dangers of the Internet: it is far too easy to post or pass along something that is frankly just in terrible taste.

Which brings me to another question for which I

still don't have a good answer. If Facebook and Twitter are all about sharing, does a repost or a retweet bear the same responsibility as an original post? And does someone who has a thousand friends bear less blame or carry any less responsibility than someone who has over a million? I have felt the pressure and increased scrutiny that comes with a growing Internet presence. It is on some level distressing to think that the more people who are paying attention, the less fun we might have together. Like I said, lowest common denominator of butthurt.

It helps that when it comes down to it, in most cases, I just don't care very much if my humor offends someone and they unlike me over it. It's even more amusing when people get huffy and post on my wall about their departure. To that, I've said the following: "Unfriending me when I didn't even know we were friends? It's like breaking wind when you're home alone. If I can't smell you, knock yourself out. #PhantomMenace."

<u>Grammar Nazis</u>

You're, your. It's, its. Their, there, they're. Are these really so difficult to distinguish and use properly?

Apparently so. On the Internet, grammatical and spelling errors abound, even with (and often because of) our friend Autocorrect. Each post affords yet another opportunity for the undereducated or the maddeningly careless to offend, mobilize and often infuriate the unofficial keepers of The Rules of English.

More ominously, each tweet, limited as they are to 140 characters or less, chips inexorably away at form in favor of function. Three spaces are gained by losing all the e's in "between" when written as "btwn." The word "tonight" becomes "tonite" or, shorter still, "2nite." Will we witness a day where the differences among "too," "two" and "to" won't matter, because they are all spelled as "2"?

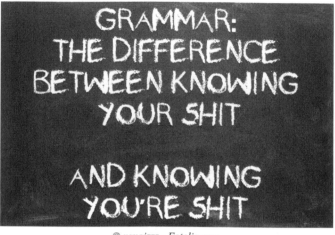

© *rangizzz - Fotolia.com.*
Used with permission.

The Netizens who keep us all on our proverbial toes are known generally as Grammar Nazis (I didn't invent the term, so my apologies if you're offended by the casual appropriation of this word). Their singular mission is to ensure that our rapid transition to a social media-based culture does not result in the wholesale destruction of The Olde Ways.

'Tis no easy feat. With everyone an author these days on social media, there are far too few properly trained and vigilant editors. Without their watchful eyes, common errors would become commonly accepted errors, and thus by the sheer weight of their misuse become simply commonly accepted. If you think I'm joking, witness how the chill-inducing and non-standard "irregardless" has crept into our speech, and even our prose, since the early twentieth century.

And so the Grammar Nazis have assumed the thankless and wearying task of monitoring the hallways of the Internet, on the lookout for a missing "o" ("this is to cool") or an extra "e" ("awe, that's so great").

How many of you are cringing right now?

One of my favorite sites on the Internet is grammarly.com. For lovers of English, this is a terrific place to peruse for good chuckles and equally satisfying head-shakers.

My personal favorite is the misused pronominal form, as in "between you and I..." — a mistake that ironically occurs when people are trying to get it right. Then there is the tricky use of the gender neutral pronoun, made famous by Sting's lyric, "If you love somebody, set them free." I still haven't gotten comfortable with that, though in the name of gender inclusiveness and non-awkward construction, I can see why we need to go this way. "If you love somebody, set him or her free" just doesn't have the same resonance or cadence.

Proper punctuation is also quite important. Missing commas can mean all the difference in the world:

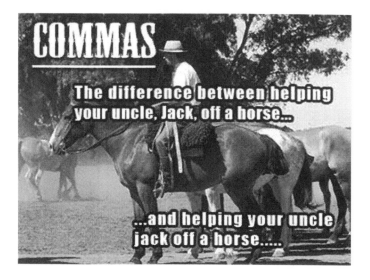

In the age of the Internet, where civil discourse frequently is reduced to a comment string on a Facebook post, the Grammar Nazis hold a decisive and rather unfair advantage. No matter how valid an opponent's point, if it contains a spelling or grammatical error, that merits instant scorn and disqualification. "The phrase is not 'myriad of ways' but 'myriad ways.' No 'of.' If you had any real education, you would know that."

Indeed, grammar correction online assumes a role not unlike name-calling. "Your English is so atrocious I don't feel the need to even respond" seems but a long-winded way of saying, "Home-schooled dumbass."

Why precisely, though, are the Grammar Nazis so keen to find and correct other people's errors? Are they fearful of the long and inevitable slide into linguistic relativism, where truth is measured solely by whether an idea has merit and not whether proper grammar is employed? I often wonder, when precisely did we concede that the rule-making was "done," and that we would all abide by a common, if misguided, set of them? After all, at some point in time the ancestors of today's Grammar Nazis huddled together in some dark room and set it all in stone. "Enough is enough," they decreed. "These are the rules, and we're sticking to them. Final answer. And while we're at it, yes, we will spell 'enough' with an 'ough' instead of a 'nuff.' Deal with it."

The loss of the semicolon as a fixture in the English language is perhaps the most galling concession the Grammar Nazis must soon face. Future generations will not recognize it as punctuation to separate two related yet complete sentences; no, its function inevitably will be reduced to a "winky eye" to be paired commonly with its cousin, the smiley close parenthesis. ;)

The Grammar Wars aren't just about spelling, conjugation or punctuation. I once ignited a fierce online debate with the simple question of whether a sentence should have two spaces after each period, or just one. It turns out, the commonly held practice today is just one — though those of us who took typing in high school (yes, typing) are so accustomed to putting two spaces after a period as a concession to courier font that old habits are hard to break. So far, however, the Grammar Nazis haven't gotten into the typesetting wars.

I would observe, however, that the QWERTY keyboard that we are all now stuck using is fixed in our culture by the same kind of thinking that Grammar Nazis employ. That is, even though they know there is a better, more rational, more efficient way to structure things, they adhere to the more cumbersome model because this is the way it has been done for so long, and there is no way they are going to change now.

I do have my moments, too. My own "pet peeve" is with the recent misuse of the word "literally." Young people are most apt to abuse this one. "I literally laughed my ass off." Did you now? I see it on you still, so how did you somehow reattach it? "The test was literally the size of a phone book." Now, which phone book was that, Monaco's?

Friends, the word "literally" means just that. It actually is, was, or did. If you mean instead to be fanciful or colorful, you must choose another word, such as "figuratively." Alternatively, you may choose none at all, and we'll all know you're being figurative. It's perfectly fine to say, simply, "I laughed my ass off." You can't be figurative if you insist you are being literal.

I confess, I love English. I make every reasonable attempt to craft my public comments within the accepted confines and strictures of Strunk and White's *The Elements of Style*. The irony of this endeavor is palpable, for English itself is a hopeless hodgepodge of other tongues, with more exceptions than rules, more chaos than order, and enough new words created each day to keep the *Oxford English Dictionary* folks very, very busy.

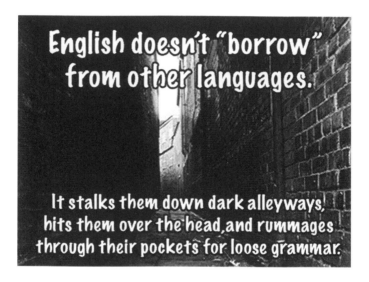

English doesn't "borrow" from other languages.

It stalks them down dark alleyways, hits them over the head, and rummages through their pockets for loose grammar.

Recently, I began seeing a great number of new words used by fans in their wall posts and comments. I thought to myself, why not see if we can bend the rules a bit more and create some new and interesting vocabulary? So I held a "new word" contest among fans, asking them to submit not only the proposed new word, but a definition and an example of how the word would be used in context. To my delight, I received over five thousand submissions!

The winning entry, voted upon by the fans themselves, was this gem:

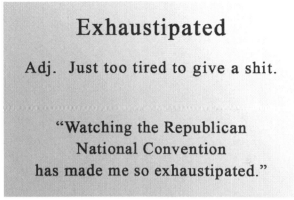

Exhaustipated

Adj. Just too tired to give a shit.

**"Watching the Republican
National Convention
has made me so exhaustipated."**

Source Credit: Michael Whittemore. Used with Permission.

Republican fans were quick to amend the meme to reflect their exhaustipation with the Democrats. The close runners-up deserve mention here as well:

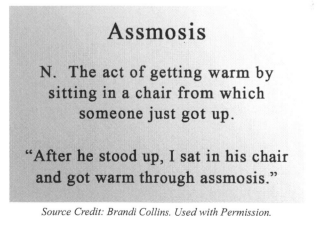

Assmosis

N. The act of getting warm by
sitting in a chair from which
someone just got up.

**"After he stood up, I sat in his chair
and got warm through assmosis."**

Source Credit: Brandi Collins. Used with Permission.

Macturbate

V. The act of pleasuring oneself through use of an Apple product.

"Steve got an iPhone5 for his birthday and has been macturbating all weekend"

Source Credit: Chris Parkes. Used with Permission.

I was tickled to learn that the good folks at the Oxford Dictionaries actually took interest in the contest and posted about it on their site:

"HERE AT OXFORD DICTIONARIES WE'RE ALWAYS MONITORING NEW WORDS AND MEANINGS FOR INCLUSION IN OUR DICTIONARIES: ONCE A WORD OR PHRASE HAS GAINED ENOUGH TRACTION, AND WE'VE RECORDED ENOUGH EVIDENCE OF ITS USAGE, WE USE OUR LANGUAGE RESEARCH TO CREATE ACCURATE DEFINITIONS.

IN TODAY'S SOCIAL, VIRTUAL, VIRAL WORLD WE'VE SEEN HOW QUICKLY NEW COINAGES AND USAGES CAN SPREAD, SO WE'RE WATCHING WITH INTEREST AS TAKEI'S FANS SUBMIT NEW WORDS IN THEIR THOUSANDS."

Oh myyy. I believe I had what they call a "nerdgasm." I hope that word has made it in, too.

So Grammar Nazis be warned: For each rule and principle you cling to with your fierce, unyielding, and yes, admirable determination, new and dynamic forces are at work that inevitably will undermine your efforts. Antecedents will dangle, prepositions will complete sentences, and infinitives will be split.

After all, it is our continuing mission "to boldly go where no one has gone before."

Chairman Meow

Somewhere along the way to the digital age, somebody decided that cats conjugate improperly when speaking English, plot the end of the human race, and love to eat cheeseburgers. For some other mysterious reason, these assumptions stuck, and a new breed of cat memes and videos made their way onto the Interweb.

I do love cats, and I actually have three. They are outdoor cats, and we've named them Fluffy, Ginger and Evil Eyes. Evil Eyes is so named because his eyes have that preternatural glow to them that only certain cats can boast. They are semi-feral creatures who live happily in our yard. Here I am feeding them. They're refusing, as cats will, to look at the camera as directed.

As much as I adore cats, my fans love them more. Factoid: There are some 86.4 million pet cats in the United States alone. This in part explains the success of the musical *Cats* (it certainly wasn't the nonexistent plot). Whenever I post an image with a cat in it, I can count on a baseline of tens of thousands of "likes" and "shares." Even if the cat is really ugly.

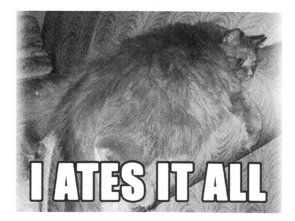

You probably know that some of the most popular videos on YouTube are cat videos. If you haven't seen the "Ninja" cat and the "Patty Cake" cats, you aren't very good at surfing the Net. There are even YouTube videos about how popular cats are on YouTube — including a hilarious one on "catvertising" that makes this very point.

© eldeiv - Fotolia.com. Used with Permission.

I've lately asked myself why we are so fascinated by cats. Much of the attraction derives from their highly human-like expressions and the rich variation in their size, color and, often, girth. We see our own exploits, frustrations, and failures in their eyes and their efforts. By contrast, dogs are commonly portrayed as "one-note" creatures that have more unconditional, simpler expressions. It also may explain why there is no musical called *Dogs*.

Take, for example, this picture:

Now, imagine an all-feline version of *Lord of the Rings*, and you can easily see this fellow in the role of Gandalf.

Note the subtlety of the performance here: the epic struggle, the sense of doom, and the bitter knowledge that nothing he can do will alter his fate as he plunges to an epic battle-to-the-death with a Balrog. Or in his case, the linoleum.

I've done some thinking on the matter, and here are a few key points about cats that might help explain their Internet dominance.

Cats fail, epically. By that I mean that cats "go for it" with gusto, then fall flat on their asses, just like the gal in the YouTube sensation "Scarlet Takes A Tumble" (Google this — it's worth it). There are innumerable clips of cats falling into bathtubs, getting stuck in small places, or leaping at ceiling fans and getting their claws caught to be spun about like a tether ball. It's like a constant loop from *Wipe Out*.

Cats are weird. They chase around little red laser lights. They make funny sounds at bugs while their little jaws quiver. And they like to sit in cardboard boxes. If you own a cat, you know what I mean. Put out a cardboard box, and your cat will sit in it.

Cats are fussy. They preen and clean incessantly like the obsessive/compulsive divas they are. They only like their food a certain way. They relieve themselves in boxes, but never while anyone is looking. And they don't like their routine or environs disturbed. Anyone who has ever tried to drive with a cat in the car knows this.

Cats are snooty. When you come home, even after a long day at work, there's a good chance your cat will look up at you, then turn away like you're the help. And like you've arrived for work late.

Cats are unpredictable. It is a fine line between the cute, inquisitive and innocent creature resting on our lap and the hissing, spitting and deranged banshee it might become at any moment. This is why we're trying always to win their love.

There is, of course, a large segment of the population that doesn't share my appreciation for cats. These individuals are, simply put, not "cat people." To them, the *felis catus* is inherently wicked or, at a minimum, demon-possessed. So while some will look at a sweet, serene face, with two placid, profoundly far-away eyes, and see the angelic spirit that the ancient Phoenicians revered, others see nothing but evil incarnate.

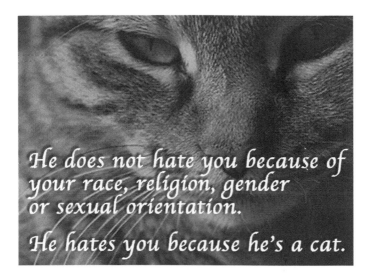

He does not hate you because of your race, religion, gender or sexual orientation.

He hates you because he's a cat.

Then there's the particularly curious question of cat grammar. On the Internet, cats are often depicted using "cute" English, with sentences like "I haz a box to pooz in" or "You hates Mondayz, toos?" To the suspicious, this supposedly adorable speech pattern simply furthers the cat's master plan, in which its owner is lulled into a false sense of quietude, as the cat patiently awaits the day when a decided lack of vigilance permits utter mayhem to ensue, no doubt later blamed upon an unsuspecting dog or small child.

For my part, I've always imagined that cats actually talk much more like Stewie or Mr. Burns, pairing a certain diabolical undertone with an overly enlarged sense of power and purpose. When a cat looks up at me, that practiced dismissal so palpable, I often hear one of those voices saying, "Another cat post, George? Really?"

Don't You Have A Bridge To Go Live Under?

When I first ventured out into the Twitterverse, I had no idea that it was filled with so many monsters. In Internet lingo, these are called "trolls." Their whole purpose in life is to ruin your good time, or as one friend puts it, to "pee in your Cheerios."

A troll is an online stalker, of sorts, who ignites passions by posting offensive, inflammatory or, perhaps most annoyingly, off-topic comments to a status update, image, video or story. Trolls are anonymous lurkers on the fringes of the Web, socially maladjusted creatures who, as they say, "have no life." They crave attention; the bigger the audience, or the more famous the target, the greater the trolls' delight. Frequently they will perch at their terminals, hurling *ad hominem* attacks and expletives in ALL CAPS, hoping to bait others into responding.

More seasoned commentators on sites like YouTube will gently remind other community members simply "not to feed the trolls" — it's our very outrage and emotion that causes them to grow stronger. But all the reminders in the world are usually for naught as, inevitably, some indignant Netizen rises to challenge the troll to an online duel. The Netizen dutifully cites evidence or studies, articulates with reason and logic, and even deploys common sense and an appeal to decency in an attempt to enlighten or transform the troll into an actual human being. The usual response to such efforts goes something like this: "WHY DON'T YOU GO OFF YOURSELF YOU PERVERT QUEER. YOU MAKE ME SICK!!!"

Pardon the troll-ese. In my earlier days spent online, before self-policing communities armed with "report" buttons were common place, trolls could rail and shriek with near impunity. On YouTube, there were legions of them in the comments left under my first few videos. While such posts could be "flagged" as inappropriate or offensive, that did not stop a troll from posting a new comment moments later. And while a troll could be, with some greater effort, banned from posting beneath a video altogether, it was easy enough for the troll to assume a new identity and return to spread his bile across the screen. I say "his" because, in my experience, trolls are mostly male. Indeed, I venture to guess that some of the most vicious trolls are repressed homosexuals, desperate to beat back their inner demons with hyper-exaggerated, outward manifestations of their professed heterosexuality.

Here is what the Internet has largely determined what a "troll" looks like:

At first, I was quite taken aback, one could even say horrified, by what I saw spewing from certain trolls' keyboards. I thought of all the young people who might be viewing, say, my "It's OK to be Takei" video, hoping to take heart in the positive message, only to skim through the comments and see so much hate and vitriol directed to them. And so I did my best to flag and delete anything that seemed like mere troll speech to me. I wanted those abusers buried, and buried for good.

But China's one-time leader, Deng Xiaoping, perhaps said it best: "When you open the window, flies and mosquitoes come in." He was talking about corruption in a Capitalist system, but the analogy works here as well. The Internet is a place where ideas compete, and bad ideas in particular get shared. There simply is no effective way to censor or limit much of anything. For starters, it would be a full-time job to monitor each and every comment on each and every video or post on each and every site. The better solution, I found, was to let the "marketplace of ideas" place its own values on the opinions expressed. Sure, it was entirely possible a good Netizen's words would be wasted on a troll, but they still might resonate with others perusing the same string. If passions were so stirred that someone had to say *something*, perhaps that was not so bad an outcome. Spread effectively, troll shit could indeed fertilize a whole crop of thinkers. Indeed, perhaps that was an unintended benefit — lemonade from the sour lemons as it were.

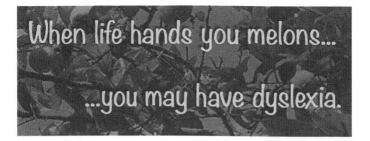

There was, of course, also the problem of where to draw the line. One fan easily could find an opinion "offensive," while others would find the very same statement a fundamental tenet of their beliefs. Well-intentioned Christians often found themselves on the defensive on my page if they entered the fray of my comment streams, especially if their church's teachings against The Gays required them to hate the sin but love the sinner. Other fans would blast them immediately, wondering why they were even on my page at all if they didn't like gay people. Now, it's a truism that once religion gets thrown in the mix, it's nearly impossible to get anyone to agree on anything. And I'm of the firm belief that you can't change any minds by closing doors; no one can break open the piñata if you ban them from the fiesta. So I decided early on that it would be better to welcome all manner of commentary and opinion across each of my social media platforms, and that I would simply not normally censor or delete as a matter of principle.

There were certain things, however, I have never felt are helpful or valuable to a robust discussion. Those include specific uses of hate speech designed to intimidate or denigrate on the basis of race, ethnicity, religion, gender, or sexual orientation — the "suspect classes" identified by our jurisprudence, based on historical patterns of discrimination or immutable characteristics. When such hate speech is directed at other fans, I do delete it and ban the author from returning. I figure, it's my Facebook page, and I make the rules. Everyone deserves to be treated with respect, and those who don't abide by that basic principle aren't welcome. Some fans cry "First Amendment" foul, but this misses the point. Facebook is not run by the government, so there aren't laws against restricting speech, particularly on one's own page. Besides, Facebook itself has a policy against such speech.

But when hate speech is directed to *me* on my own page, I more often than not leave it as is. Such speech doesn't have any power over me. I've simply been around too long, and been through too much, to let a few words from an anonymous coward get to me. But I do find that such hate speech serves as a terrific rallying cry for my defenders. I'll tell you, nothing feels better than to see legions of fans call out a jerk on my behalf.

Apart from the most hateful trollspeak, there is a lesser and more common form of "trolling" where one merely seeks to get a "rise" out of others. I admit, I have designed some of my own posts to have this very effect. I know, for example, that any time I post anything that pits men against women, particularly one that plays upon a stereotype, it will surely create a maelstrom.

A man is like Bluetooth:

Connecting when close, but

searching for other devices

when you aren't nearby...

A woman is like Wi-Fi:

Seeing all available devices, but

connecting with the strongest one.

Such posts are bound to stir the pot, and I'm always ready to be barraged with emails and comments accusing me of perpetuating stereotypes. People forget that stereotypes aren't bad because they are always untrue. Stereotypes are bad because they are not *always* true. If we allow ourselves to judge another based on a stereotype, we have allowed a gross generalization to replace our own thinking. Therein lies the problem.

But if we fail to acknowledge or, God forbid, laugh at a dubious stereotype, then we do ourselves a disservice. I much prefer to identify and open up the discussion of the stereotype than to pretend it doesn't exist.

My brand of "trolling" thus has almost the exact opposite intent of a traditional troll. I wish to provoke enlightened and spirited discussion, not shut it down. When I turn over a rock and cause the Internet bugs to wiggle, it is to prevent intellectual laziness from taking hold — the very kind of laziness that gives stereotypes power in the marketplace.

Plus, to be honest, it's just a lot of fun to turn over those rocks and see what is crawling around underneath.

But Enough About Me. What Do YOU Think of Me?

When most people use Facebook or Twitter, they post about their own lives. They put it out there, hoping that others will find their lives compelling enough to follow. Each small victory or triumph matters; each event becomes a gem of a memory. Otherwise, why create status updates at all?

As I mentioned at the beginning of this book, celebrities talk about their lives too. They, or more likely their handlers, often treat social media as just another way to market themselves, as if it were simply a new kind of broadcast media. Their tweets and updates are often creative agency pre-packaged bits about upcoming appearances, performances and whatnot.

While some fans appreciate this information, this really is not a great way to engage them. Only the most die-hard, dutiful fans will like, comment, or retweet what are essentially commercials. And very few friends of those fans will pay such reposts any heed. They know that all that giddiness is just their friends "fan boying" or "fan girling" out.

I make no bones about my intentions on Facebook and other platforms. I've got some things I'd like to say about the world, particularly in the area of civil rights, and I'd love it if a lot of people got to hear them. I realize that there just aren't many folks my age reaching out on the Internet, so I understand that my position comes with a certain level of responsibility.

I also want a lot of people to laugh, or even better, to laugh with me. The world is far too grim a place without some daily guffaws. Some of my favorite fan posts come from regular folks who tell me that they were having a bad day, or going through a rough time, but my page made them laugh, and that helped keep them going. I can't express how grateful that makes me feel in turn, that I can make a difference, however small, in so many people's daily lives.

But in all honesty, there's no way millions of fans, particularly millions of young fans, would bother to get to know me unless I talked about something other than myself and my gigs. There are only so many *Star Trek* conventions and symphony narrations that anyone can take. Many of the younger fans probably have never even been to a symphony given the cost of tickets. And honestly, I also worry about people knowing *exactly* where I am or what I'm up to at all hours.

Common sense suggests I shouldn't tell the world, for example, that I'm out of town with Brad, please come rob our home. Because of this, I'll usually post any personal pictures well after the fact. It only takes one disturbed "fan" to ruin the party and cost me a lot in lost sleep and added security detail.

So, from the outset, I resisted the urge to fill my page with me, me, me. This wasn't a hard choice, because much of my life is pretty mundane. I also eschewed attempts to sell copies of my existing book, much to Brad's initial displeasure.

All kidding aside, it may come as a surprise to many, but peddling a product or service right out of the box doesn't really work that well as an online strategy. Facebook in particular is a pretty lousy place to sell something, because people really aren't on Facebook looking to buy. They're looking to be entertained.

By "entertained" I don't mean in the traditional sense of television. People on Facebook want to feel connected. In some ways, the experience online is more like live entertainment, akin to being at the theater or in the studio audience of a TV comedy. In addition to the energy you're taking in from the performer, there's the unquantifiable connectedness you feel with the audience around you. Facebook is a place, then, not only where you can laugh, wonder or curse at a video or image, but add your own thoughts and share in the thoughts of others immediately, in a kind of collective intelligence.

Yes, I know, it's hard to say "collective" without thinking of the Borg.

To say simply that content is king when it comes to social media therefore misses half the point. You need content, yes, but it has to reflect the collective sensibilities of the fans, not just the imperatives or tastes of the entertainer. I believe it's crucial to understand audience aspirations, commonalities and sensitivities, and to deliver the fans what they want. Only then will you have any chance of them giving a rat's ass about what you have to say.

My Facebook page, you might say then, is basically a place where I post things that my *fans* like. That sounds simple, but many celebrities and brands have a hard time understanding this. Most people simply don't care about the 10K race you sponsored. Instead, I'd prefer to put up a picture of a kid running it with prosthetic legs, and make that the focal point of a post.

Few of my posts are truly about me or my opinions. In fact, I've found that some fans have taken this principle a bit too far to heart. These fans' feathers get quite ruffled whenever I happen to post something that relates directly to me, or I should say more specifically, my opinions. There are many examples of this. After the first Presidential debate between Obama and Romney, I posted an image of an armed gang of Muppets, furious that Romney had threatened to cancel *Sesame Street*, and openly declaring, "Shit just got real." I found the picture wickedly funny, not only because Elmo, Grover and Cookie Monster were armed with knives, but also because they were paired with such a colorful caption.

I wasn't prepared for the backlash from Romney supporters, who were more numerous than I'd assumed existed on what is essentially a liberal page. "Why don't you C-list celebrities keep your opinions to yourselves?" "I liked this page for its humor, not liking it so much now for its politics." "Shut up and keep to being funny, Mr. Takei. Don't be so misinformed."

Apparently, some fans can't take a joke if it happens to bash their candidate. But being a person who normally wants to find the common ground beneath our many heels, I was bothered by the comments. There was something highly presumptuous about the criticism. They assumed I was not free to post whatever I wanted to on my own page. For starters, they insisted that it was my job to spend my free time making them laugh, with no thought to my own wants or needs.

I felt the rare need this time to respond, not only to make it clear that I took issue with these presumptions, but also because I knew it would only become worse with what I was about to post. You see, I had been approached earlier by the Obama campaign to record a couple of endorsement videos that encouraged Asian Pacific Islanders and LGBT individuals to get out and vote. I knew that a sizeable and vocal portion of my own fan base held different political beliefs than my own, ranging from Independent to Republican to Libertarian. Many were clearly not fans of the President and were eager to see him defeated. By using my fan page as a bully pulpit, even for a few posts, I was certain to see backlash.

And so I put out a simple and rare personal statement:

George Takei
October 5 via mobile

Some have written complaining that I share more than mere laughs on this page. Indeed, I do have opinions. So do most of you. I invite all to share theirs, as I share mine from time to time. Do so with respect and tolerance, and all are welcome.

Like · Comment · Share   797

147,433 people like this.

View previous comments   2 of 11,978

Terminal Velocity You are a great man for being so accepting of the blatant stupidity and ignorance that runs ramped on facebook. My Hats off to you Sir. I still think you should have had a little more face time as a Captain, I think you are one of the best only Second the the Shat. LOL
31 minutes ago · Like · 1

Klaus Hillingmeier 100% correkt!!!
2 minutes ago · Like

Write a comment...

2,076,386 people saw this post   Promote ▼

I was thrilled to see the response of the fans, with over 147,000 fans clicking like on it and over 10,000 commenting, nearly all positive. The people had spoken: This is George Takei's page, and he can say whatever he damn well pleases!

But part of the risk of carefully growing a cohesive online community is that the cohesion can prove illusory, giving way quickly in the face of divisive politics or beliefs. Although I was quite proud of them and knew that they could move many viewers to action, my endorsement videos were, shall I say, not welcomed by a certain percentage of my fan base. It didn't matter that I had prefaced the first post as tactfully as I could imagine:

I did take the time, as I usually do, to read through a great deal of the comments below my posts. To my dismay, most of the 4000+ comments expressed on the first video expressed disappointment; indeed many were highly critical. Hundreds questioned how I could speak so passionately in the video about how my family was incarcerated in camps during World War II simply because we were of Japanese descent, yet support a President who had signed into law the National Defense Authorization Act (NDAA) — a provision in which grants him the very power of indefinite detention without trial that I had just condemned. For the record, I had blogged about my opposition to the NDAA earlier and was dismayed that the President had signed it. It had been passed by veto-proof majority of 93 out of 100 senators, which may explain but doesn't excuse his signature.

So this wasn't just a case of shaking the tree and having a lot of nuts fall down. Thousands of my fans on the opposite end of the political spectrum were genuinely upset and were citing valid concerns. While I was happy that my "push" on my Facebook page ultimately lifted the number of YouTube views on the first video to over 175,000, I couldn't help but feel like I'd pulled a Sinead O'Connor on some lesser scale (you might recall, on *Saturday Night Live* Ms. O'Connor had ended a performance by ripping a picture of the Pope in half — a highly controversial statement that cost her significant goodwill with many fans, some of who began booing her at concerts).

But another part of me was upset that I had somehow managed to turn myself into some kind of Internet personality who wasn't allowed to have real world opinions anymore. Every engaged adult citizen has the right to vote in this country, and all of us are supposed to be guaranteed freedom of speech. How could the Internet manage to censor, through public opprobrium, what the government itself had no power to silence? Was I to curtail my own outspoken nature in order to keep a portion of my fans on board?

It struck me that, in the minds of many fans, I am an actor and an entertainer, and it is therefore presumptuous of me to use whatever popularity I have to push a social or political agenda. This is why Richard Gere's decision to talk about Tibet on the Oscars raised a collective sigh of exasperation. Actors aren't any smarter than anyone else, so the thinking goes, they're just more popular. But their fans made them popular so they could make movies and TV shows, not so they could lecture the world.

So let me be clear. I am an actor, yes, but I am also an activist. Indeed, the "golden" years of my life have been marked more by the latter than the former. As I write this book, I am starring in a musical called *Allegiance* which I consider my legacy project. *Allegiance* is set during World War II and the Japanese American internment, and it's the first time such a story will be told on the Broadway stage. I want this story told because I want it remembered.

The internment, you see, was not just a Japanese American story; it was an American one. It was the

U.S. Constitution that was violated by the detention of over 120,000 persons of Japanese decent, without charge or trial, and it was our nation's promise of due process that was eviscerated. One of the reasons I believe *Allegiance* will succeed, where other internment stories have failed, is that it entertains as well as educates. It lifts the spirit, its music soars, and our hearts break together, actors and audience, as we participate in the story eight times a week.

I truly hope my social media work has the same ultimate effect. Sure, it's primarily entertaining, but it's also educational. I want people to not only laugh, but to think, to not only be inspired, but to participate. Fans may not always agree with me, but they will know I have an opinion, as will they, I'm sure. My Facebook page will remain a place where those opinions are hashed out freely and openly on the Internet.

How do you start an online argument? 1. Post something.

About a week later, I released my second Obama

endorsement video, joining with Jesse Tyler Ferguson, Jane Lynch, Wanda Sykes, Billie Jean King, Chaz Bono and Zachary Quinto in praising the administration for its strides forward on the question of LGBT equality. I told the story of how moved I was to hear the President say that he believed gays and lesbians should be allowed to marry. And I expressed my firm belief that we have to keep fighting for our rights, which means not supporting the party that would take us backwards — in this case, the Republican ticket.

It came as no surprise that this second endorsement video raised another hoopla, though smaller than the first. It seems my fan base is less surprised that I would endorse Obama on account of his stance on gay rights than on account of his support for the Asian American community. Or perhaps the fans have just gotten more used to me speaking my mind on a political matter. I began to feel a bit of what the candidates themselves must feel each time they take a position that threatens to alienate their base. Ultimately, you must take a position, and accept the consequences of that decision, even if it means losing some support. If people truly support you, they'll come back around, and even hold their nose and vote for you (or in my case, reluctantly start clicking like and sharing my funnies again).

It may seem I've gone full circle, arguing that to build a fan base it has to be about them, but to reach them with any kind of message, you have to be willing to sometimes make it about you. I suppose in the end it's all about the balance and the timing. Fans will forgive the occasional self-promotion (after all, it's what's selling this book) and even forgive the politics in a political season. As far as I can tell, few of my fans "unfollowed" me for the sin of expressing my opinion, and if they did, well, I hope they miss the laughs and come back. I'll keep the light on for them.

Spider-man, Spider-man, George Takei should be Spider-man

I've come to understand, in a small way, the demands that humanity puts on its superheroes. Allow me to explain.

The producers of *Allegiance* approached me with the idea that we should do a video series called, "The Road to Broadway," with me auditioning for various shows currently playing. I thought it sounded like a splendid idea. We were years away from our own Broadway debut, but I understood that to get there, we needed to build buzz early for the show. So I was all for it.

Then they told me that the first show I would make a video about was *Spider-man: Turn Off the Dark*. Now, if you haven't been paying attention, *Spider-man* on Broadway is a multi-million dollar extravaganza that was plagued from the outset with numerous technical difficulties and injuries, some very serious. So I wasn't sure how I was going to pull off my own Peter Parker. "Don't worry," they assured. "We'll do everything on green screen, and we'll have professional stunt people there to help."

When I got to the sound studio, I learned that I would be spending much of my day in a body harness, dangling several feet off the ground. Now, this may not sound like that big of an ordeal, but try doing that after over seventy years spent with your feet mostly on the ground. I had done some of my own stunts for my appearances on NBC's *Heroes*, including one where I had to lie on my stomach — on a body-form pedestal — nearly horizontally in mid-air with my arms and legs suspended by thin wires for quite some time, and I knew how exhausting it could be.

My Spidey costume was something our production assistant had purchased online as a one-size-fits-all, so to make it look like I wasn't wearing a pillowcase, it had to be stretched taut around my arms and legs and safety-pinned in the back. Brad, who is used to dealing with such last-minute fixes, set out immediately to find some pins, while I practiced singing the theme song: "Spider-man, Spider-man, George Takei should be Spider-man!" I wanted to prove I really had the chops for a Broadway audition.

The truly hilarious moment came when they finally

got the harness on me. It accentuated, shall we say, certain parts of my body that no one had expected. You see, the straps came under each leg right around the crotch and tended to push everything else forward.

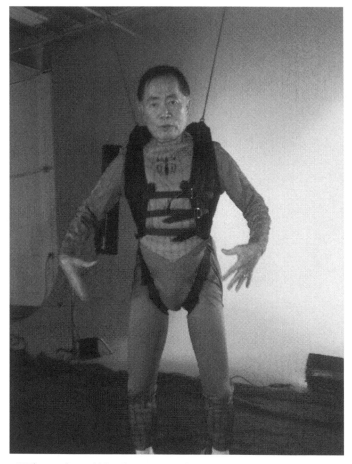

When they lifted me up, there was an embarrassed

silence for about five seconds before the entire team burst out laughing. It was decidedly absurd. But the producers loved it, so rather than adjust the harness (or get me some kind of dance belt), we decided instead to run with it, adding a line to have me say, "As you can see, I've got the whole package!"

There was another unexpectedly hilarious aspect of this. Once I was airborne, there was no way to predict which direction I would be facing. So I literally had to "swim" my way around to face forward. The mechanics of that were so awkward that, again, the producers decided to use it to underscore the absurdity of the shot.

The video[1] has me fending off some super-villains, all of whom were played by the same volunteer (thank you, David Rae from Los Angeles). Because we were improvising the way the hoist was positioning me, the fight choreography was also something we had to invent on the spot, and given our budget, had to shoot again and again from different angles.

In the next page you can see some of my favorite screen shots from the video.

---

1   http://www.allegiancemusical.com/video/road-broadway-ep-i

On occasion, the choreographers and our director (a talented young man named Ryan James Yezak who has made many terrific short films on behalf of the LGBT community) would consult on how to achieve the next sequence without killing or injuring me, forgetting that I was still dangling in the air above them. After a minute or two, I'd have to remind them with a gentle, "Can I please come down for a few?" (The crew later told me that I actually had been a terrific sport about it all, and that by comparison another better known actor who had recently worked with the crew, and who was known for his tough-guy image, would complain every few seconds about being left dangling. Let's just say his name rhymes with Snarky Snark.)

I don't think the world was quite ready to see me as Spider-man. When the video launched, nearly every major blog picked up the story, as well as much of the mainstream entertainment media. It wasn't clear if this was so epic that it had to be seen...or so awful. Either way, the producers had hit upon a great combination — someone of my years going out for one of the most dangerous roles on Broadway. Nobody seemed to mind that it essentially was a gigantic advertisement for our show, done in an entertaining and subversive way. I still get fan mail asking whether I got the part. After all, as I told the viewers, not only do I have great vocals, I've got great insurance.

My second "Road to Broadway" video had me cross-dressing. I portrayed "Sister Mary Teriyaki," and I was bent on crashing the set and joining the cast of *Sister Act* on Broadway.

Of course, we shot the whole thing in Los Angeles, and edited in footage (actually from the London production of *Sister Act*) to make it look like I was there. Ah, the magic of green screen!

While this shoot proved to be far less technically demanding than *Spider-man* (I didn't have to spend any time in a body harness), I had to brush up on my vocals. To sing the part in the show's signature number "Raise Your Voice," I had to memorize a real tongue-twister of a lyric: *"Laudamus te; benedicimus te; adoramus te; glorificamus te...."* Try saying that a few times fast. And I had to do this trying not to laugh at how I looked in a wimple.

The producers also wanted me to show off my deep bass at the end of the video by shattering a glass, solely using my voice. No really, that's what they wanted. Of course, it was all a big stunt. They had provided me with a prop "magic" glass which I held in my hand, and which I could shatter with just the slightest pressure. I was assured it posed no danger to me, but it was still a challenge to make it appear as if the vibrations of my voice alone did the work. So I let loose with a deep "aaaaaaah" and broke the sucker — and we got it all in one shot. Oh, Maaaary!

I haven't had a chance to do a third video, but I'm looking forward to what the producers select. Perhaps I should play a missionary for *The Book of Mormon* or don an animal mask for *The Lion King*.

Apart from my "Road to Broadway" series, I've

also enjoyed doing what I call "public service announcement" videos. Back in the day, on *Jimmy Kimmel Live*, I called out NBA star Tim Hardaway for his homophobic remarks by facetiously threatening to have gay sex with him. I suppose that set the stage for my future videos that lampooned other anti-gay individuals. My favorite among these was my "It's OK to be Takei" piece.

A bit of background. A bill proposed in the Tennessee Legislature by Representative Stacey Campbell would have prohibited the teaching in elementary schools of even so much as the existence of homosexuality. The bill was quickly dubbed the "Don't Say Gay" bill because it proscribed even the very mention of gay people. To me, this was not only an egregious violation of equal rights, but also a suppression of the right of free speech. It was premised on the misguided belief that gay people could be silenced, and made to disappear, if no one could talk about us. Inherent in its sweep was the presumption that gays were bad people, and that children therefore could be kept from knowing about us. On a deeper level, it restricted our right to participate in civil society by closing the doors of the classroom to us and our causes, such as marriage equality or the right to adopt.

When I heard about this, I felt I had to speak out,

but in a way that would bring the right amount of public disdain upon this proposed law. So I first put out the following tweet:

TN bill will prevent teachers from using the word "gay" in class. In response, I'm lending them my name: "It's okay to be Takei."

Based on the immediate virality of that initial tweet, I knew I was on to something. So with the help of my *Allegiance* production team, I put together a video. If teachers and children were forbidden to say "gay," they could simply say "Takei." You could proclaim yourself a supporter of Takei marriage, march in a Takei pride parade, and at the holidays even sing, "Don we now our Takei apparel!"

But I wanted to do more than just get out the word on this awful bill. I wanted those who opposed it to be able to support those who would actually help defeat it. So I did what other causes do: I sold swag. The "It's OK to be Takei" line featured t-shirts, hats, mugs and buttons, with all of the proceeds donated to charities, including education funds for LGBT causes.

The video went viral beyond my wildest expectations, with over a million hits. I was particularly surprised when MSNBC's Rachel Maddow picked up the story, naming me and the campaign the "Best New Thing in the World" on her show. Oh myyy. You can see the whole video at youtube.com/watch?v=dRkI-WB3HIEs

The video helped bring attention to this ridiculous law, but the Tennessee legislature was far from done. Within a year, they proposed two other outrageous bills. One protected bullies who target LGBT youth by making an exception for acts committed in the name of "religious freedom." The second, targeted towards transgendered people, would make it a criminal offense to use any public facility designated for a gender other than what appears on your birth certificate. The sponsor threatened publicly to "stomp a mud hole" through any transgendered person coming near his family.

I again felt compelled to respond. In a second video, which I modeled after the fireside chats of President Franklin Delano Roosevelt, I suggested that these three lawmakers were like certain "friends of Dorothy," in that they lacked brains, heart and courage. So I got gifts for each of them, hoping to help their situation: an "It's OK to be Takei" shirt for the author of the "Don't Say Gay" law, whose bill was a true straw man; for the author of the bully protection law, a copy of *Twilight* — a movie so "Takei" that even his heartless soul couldn't help but flutter; and for the author of the transgendered bathroom prohibition, a gift certificate to women's clothier Lane Bryant, in the hope he could find the courage to be who he really is on the inside. You can see the full video at http://vimeo.com/38068014

I don't know ultimately whether my videos changed any minds within the Tennessee legislature. What I do know is that they helped bring national attention to local tomfoolery, and that all three bills failed to get to a full vote on the floor. For that, I'm grateful.

In taking on certain Tennessee state legislators, however, I set for myself quite a precedent, one that I fear will be hard to match. So many states and municipalities have become embroiled in controversy, particularly over marriage equality, that I am asked almost daily to lend my voice and support (or opposition, as the case may be) to ballot measures, initiatives, pending legislation, or political struggles. It seemed the LGBT cause needed a new hero, but I wasn't sure I was its guy. This is all very new for me, because suddenly I have what I call a responsibility

135

of numbers; the more "numbers" of fans, the more I know I can make a real difference. But not all of us are built to be real superheroes. I may have donned a Spidey outfit and taken on some bad guys, and I may have even thumbed my nose at small-minded legislators in Tennessee. But will my style of activism, coupled as it is with a particularly quirky sense of humor, be able to carry the day with greater causes, and before larger audiences?

I already know that many fans prefer that I stay on the sidelines, and stick to acting and making people laugh. They prefer to see me as an affable good sport, not someone out to make a real difference. But they might have to get used to seeing more of "activist" me around. Once you put on a superhero outfit, you start to feel like you really can take on the world's villains.

By the Numbers

When I first started posting my miscellany online, I had only one number to keep track of — Twitter followers. At the time, I didn't have a Facebook account, though there was a fan page on Facebook that someone else had created using my name with something on the order of 20,000 "likes." In the early going, it was rather like a game to see how many more people each day had clicked "follow" on Twitter, and to pay attention to things like my "Klout" score — which purports to measure influence across the Interwebs, but really feels more like a constant source of collective judgment.

The clever folks behind the social media curtain have managed to "game-ify" the whole experience, meaning we all are tempted to check the leader-boards. Having raw numbers at your disposal means you can quantify, at any time, how well fans are responding to you. Indeed, when I reached certain milestones, it felt like a big achievement, not unlike going up a level on a video game. I know I felt that way at my first 100,000 Twitter followers. I could hardly believe so many people actually cared to hear what I had to say on a daily basis.

Fast-forward nearly two years later, and what a difference the numbers make. It's true, I'm mostly about Facebook these days, though I do have an account on Tumblr and the picture-sharing site Pinterest where I keep more of my favorite photos, and occasionally I'll check in with the geeks over at Google+ or with my followers on Twitter. But on Facebook, with over three million fans as I write this, it's hard to even compare those early days with the frenzy a single post can create today.

Facebook has gotten into the metrics game, too, encouraging pages like mine to "bring our game" by providing daily statistics on fan growth, virality, and reach. I also receive a weekly email update of how many new fans I have, and how many have been "talking about" me during the week — meaning people who clicked "like" on my page or one of my posts, commented on or wrote something on my page, or shared content. Lately, that number has actually been exceeding the total number of fans I have, indicating there are folks out there who are participating on the page without even becoming actual fans.

I've come to understand that it's not the total number of fans that matters so much as how "engaged" they are with my page. Justin Bieber may have many more fans than I do, but on the question of engagement, I've got the Biebs beat hands down most weeks. In fact, my Webmaster told me the other day that my page often rises to hold the title of second most popular "personal" page on Facebook. "Well, what's the first?" I heard my Asian parents asking in my head. Turns out it's something called "Jesus Daily" — a collection of affirmatory and inspirational posts that, you guessed it, come out daily about our Savior. I suppose I'm just fine playing second fiddle to Jesus.

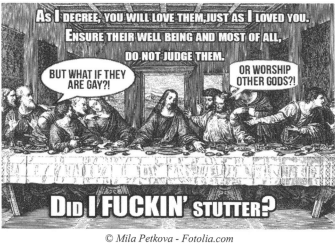

© Mila Petkova - Fotolia.com
Used with Permission

Beyond the "talking about" number, which measures fan engagement, there's also something called the "weekly total reach" (which is an incomprehensible 30 million as I write this). That refers to how many other people, meaning presumably friends of fans, actually saw something I posted. Then there's the more nebulous "friends of friends" stat, which is way up in some stratospheric number of 226 million. I'm not exactly sure what Facebook wishes to convey with that number, other than that there really are only six degrees to Kevin Bacon, but the gist is that a lot of potential people can now see the same post through viral sharing.

I was most delighted to learn that when Facebook wanted to create a graphical representation of how a post goes viral, they selected some of my own posts to use as examples. I'll describe one of them. Around the time of the landing of *Curiosity* on Mars, a fan left this on my wall as the first picture taken from the rover:

I shared it right away, and when I checked it the next day, it had received over 100,000 likes (timing, I've found, is the key to breaking six figures). Facebook went back and actually mapped how the post went viral. I'm represented in the center of this fractal-like image:

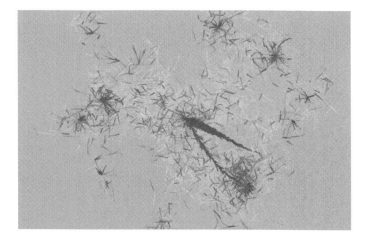

You can see an animated version of this at www.vimeo.com/50730773

You can see that "my" virality depends also in large part on certain other unspecified centers, where much later activity occurs. I imagine these might be other blogs or pages that follow my page, who have thousands or even millions of their own fans. It's truly remarkable to contemplate how connected we all are, and how quickly a thought or image can now spread.

Using Facebook "Insights" I can delve deeper and see where my fans are located, not only by country, but even by city. It's no surprise that my biggest fan base is my hometown of Los Angeles. I can also see how old they are, what gender they are, and, principally, what languages they speak. Looking at those numbers is a heady experience, and I'm especially grateful for all of the overseas fans who participate in English on my page.

Having relatively high numbers also means that I get to play all sorts of fun games on friends. I particularly enjoy dropping what I call "Facebombs" on my colleagues. One example was the actor Telly Leung, who stars alongside me in *Allegiance*. I play the older version of Telly's character, Sam Kimura, in the present day; he plays the younger version of me in the 1940s. On Telly's birthday, I wanted to surprise him by sending fans over to his page. At the time, he had some 2,000 Facebook fans — a respectable number for a young up-and-coming actor. Then came the Facebomb. I asked my fan base to do me the honor of clicking "Like" on Telly's page, and to see whether we could double his number to 4,000. Within half an hour, he had jumped to over 5x the original number, and his wall was filled with well-wishers, saying that George had sent them. I was delighted that fans were willing to play along, and Telly was astonished to now have over 10,000 fans.

I played a similar game with the producers of *Allegiance*, who had painstakingly built their fan page from zero to around 140,000 fans. During our run, they had hoped that fan interest would push their numbers higher, so I bet them a round of drinks that

I could get them past 200,000. They were admittedly skeptical. But with just two nudges to my very loyal fans, the numbers jumped almost 25,000 in a single day.

So I doubled down: "I'll bet you another round of drinks you'll have 250,000 by Opening Night." We started the bet at around 165,000 fans and, at first, it seemed I had bitten off more than I could comfortably chew. Fans who had been willing to go to bat for me appeared to have already signed up as *Allegiance* fans, and it seemed the rest couldn't be bothered. We were hovering around 180,000 fans but had stalled out. So I did what I had to do. I begged.

"I don't like to lose," I told fans. "But I bet the producers another round of drinks that I could get us to 250,000 by Opening Night." Well, that shameless plea did the trick, and we soared past 250,000 before the curtain rose on Opening Night. And I got a free round of drinks, something they were more than happy to spring for.

There is certainly a more serious side to having an ever-growing number of fans. Every day, I am asked by dozens of people to lend my help or influence to any number of incredibly worthy causes. But because of my busy schedule, I have to turn down nearly every invitation to speak, and there aren't enough posts in the day to be able to even accommodate one-tenth of the requests I receive. I hope that fans and activists understand that, when it comes down to it, I now have to pick my battles or risk losing both credibility and effectiveness should I support too many causes.

These causes go far beyond LGBT rights or reminding fans about the injustices of the Japanese American internment. Almost daily, I'm asked by fans to publicize events, groups or campaigns, to help find lost children by putting out a nationwide Amber alert, or even send well-wishers by the thousands to the page of someone terminally ill, in the hopes that positive support will make the difference. I did this once, and it had a tremendous positive effect, but it opened the door to dozens and dozens of similar requests. I have had many long discussions with Brad about how much of my page should be devoted to causes I'd like to champion, knowing full well that to continue to reach a lot of people, I can't make this my own soap box all the time.

On the other hand, the numbers of engaged fans willing to help out with my pet projects could result in some powerful results. I launched my first crowd-funded initiative on a site called Indiegogo. The producers of *Allegiance* and I hoped to raise $50,000 to help fund the show. I had no idea whether fans would respond, and they told me privately that if we raised even $20,000 they'd consider it a win. In fact, they picked Indiegogo over Kickstarter precisely because with Indiegogo, you don't have to raise your goal completely before any actual funds are collected.

All of us underestimated the enthusiasm and generosity of the fans. Within a week we sailed past our $50,000 goal, with some fans even donating $1,000 or even $5,000 to help make *Allegiance* happen. As we approached $100,000 I told the fans that I would do something special if we got there: my "Happy Dance" — something normally Brad only gets the privilege of seeing. Lo' and behold, in six shakes of a lamb's tail, we wound up raising over $158,000 for the show. I could hardly believe it. While this was still only enough to cover a small portion of what we would need, it helped tremendously, and perhaps more importantly, I proved that crowd-sourced funding really worked with my fans. Oh, and I did do my Happy Dance. Here's a shot from that:

You can see the whole dance at www.youtube.com/watch?v=cSjO-rWMuJo

Amazingly, even this video now has something on the order of 870,000 views, which I'm pleased to note means even more people have heard about our show.

Because of the success of that crowd-funding effort, I quickly became bombarded with requests to support other projects. I've had to turn all but a few of these down, mostly because I don't want my fans to feel "charity fatigue" every time they log in. But on occasion I will stumble upon something that truly moves me, and I'm compelled to lend a hand. This happened specifically with a wonderful video made by a young man, Shane Britney Crone, who had lost his life partner to a terrible accident. Shane created a YouTube video in memory of his love, and to highlight the unfairness of how Shane was kept from attending his partner's funeral services by a family that didn't accept their relationship, even though they had been together as a couple for six years.

Shane wrote to me and told me he needed help raising the final funds for a documentary he wanted to make about his story, entitled *Bridegroom*. The Kickstarter campaign had stalled on funding at around $150,000, only half of what they needed to raise, and he was worried that his project would go unfunded.

When I learned he would be working with acclaimed producer Linda Bloodworth-Thomason of *Designing Women*, I was impressed, and I felt the project could use a bit of what Brad calls the "Takei" bump.

In all, I posted twice about *Bridegroom*, and once again, I could hardly believe the results. It became the most funded documentary movie ever on Kickstarter, with well over $300,000 raised. Shane and Linda wrote wonderful emails to me, thanking for the help, but it is really my fans who I have to thank for stepping up. All I can really provide is a shot of fuel; the project has to merit support on its own to garner this kind of backing. Shane is now traveling the world speaking about the film and being honored for raising awareness of the issue. While it can never erase the pain of losing a beloved partner and of being so heartlessly denied his emotional, if not legal, rights, I hope the success of his film will bring him some solace and closure. I look forward to attending the premiere, and I hope it does well at all the film festivals.

More recently, I joined forces with Humans of New York and Tumblr to raise funds for victims of Hurricane Sandy. In addition to publicizing the campaign on my social media platforms, I donated a special portrait of me "On Broadway." Apparently, $300,000 seems to be the magic number for me, because by the end of the fundraiser on Thanksgiving Day, we had raised in excess of $318,000 together.

But for every *Bridegroom* or Hurricane Sandy relief effort, there are dozens and dozens of regrets I have to send. It saddens me to no end to have to turn people down; in fact, most of the time I don't even have the resources or staff to respond to them, and I worry that they think I am being cold or aloof. Some have even "unfriended" me because I failed to respond or took no action. I understand the hurt here; each of us has a passion project, and it's hard to accept that others may not share the same commitment or be willing to devote the same time and resources.

In a perfect world, I'd like nothing more than to be able to help all who ask. Because that's not possible, I'm now in the process of "systematizing" some of this, so that perhaps once a quarter I can help out somewhere, perhaps by having fans submit their wishes or requests to my interns, who can sort it all out. I may even have to, gulp, start hiring people to help.

The way things are going, I will need to make some changes. At present, my Facebook page gains between 25,000 and 50,000 new fans a week. I'm told that people click "like" after their friends shared repeatedly from my wall. "I'm not a Trekkie, but so many of my friends share your images, I've come to join the party" is a common theme. I don't know how long these numbers can, or will, continue to rise, but I am very much enjoying the ride. People on the street stop me now as much for my Facebook page as for my work on *Star Trek* or *Howard Stern*. It's a strange honor to be recognized simply for sharing what is largely other people's material, but I've come to recognize that people appreciate a good laugh more than almost anything. And so as long as they keep coming and sharing with me, I'll keep putting it out there for them.

Apocalypse Soon

Maybe it's because we live in a more cynical, post-9/11 world, or maybe it's because we have all seen too many post-apocalyptic movies, but my fans are decidedly and irretrievably obsessed with the end of the world. Any post I make relating to our collective destruction is sure to gain a following and to be shared avidly among the soon-to-be destroyed. We are all doom and gloom, and loving every bit of it.

The year 2012 was a particularly fertile time for the apocalypse-burdened. I blame the Maya principally for this. An aside: I learned that the correct term is "Maya" and not "Mayan," which apparently refers only to the language. The incorrect term is in such common usage, however, that people often don't know what I'm talking about if I use "Maya."

I once had the great privilege of visiting the ruins of a Maya temple in Tikal, Guatamala. It was a *Star Trek* cruise that took us down the Mexican coast. To get to the ruins, we had to board a specially chartered, very rickety aircraft, which ominously piped in the music from *Titanic* as we climbed to cruising altitude.

Tikal blew away all apprehensions over that flight. It was astounding. Built some 2,500 years ago, central Tikal covers about six miles. Looming up out of the tangle of dense jungle growth, awe-inspiring in their majesty, stood the ruins of four temple structures. Their bases were not pyramids but steeply slanted stepped shafts that soared up to a terrace in the sky. Imposingly ensconced on top were the ornately carved stone temples of the Maya high priests. Climbing to the top was, literally, a breath-taking workout. Many in our group didn't even attempt it. A friend named Cecily Adams, actress and daughter of actor Don Adams, fit athlete that she was, made it to the top with me. Here we are, pictured together in this admittedly grainy picture from that trip. Cecily tragically passed from cancer at age 46 in 2004.

Photo by Brad Altman

George Takei and Cecily Adams

The view from that spectacular vantage was as breathtaking as the climb. Below was the great central plaza where the ritual ceremonies were held. Across the way were the other temple structures. And surrounding us all was the jungle that had claimed these awesome edifices when the Maya nation mysteriously vanished. It boggled the mind to realize that this amazing civilization was built without the use of the wheel.

As most of us somehow have become aware, the Maya calendar only goes "up to" 2012. It is also based on lunar cycles, so the final, approximate date of their calendar falls on the winter solstice, 12/21/12. This not only looks like an ominous number, but is curiously just one month away from the date I am writing this. Dum-dum!!

The Maya were keen on making predictions about the future, usually about the weather and such. Depending on whom you believe, they also apparently loved to consort with alien life forms and build temples with amazing astronomical significance. Those temple builders probably knew they would have us all fretting thousands of years later, and had a good laugh over making particularly ominous markings. One popular comic strip that I reposted showed a Maya stonecutter explaining that there was only room on his sun disc to go up to 2012 and predicting that it was going to mess a lot of people up one day.

As I write this, it occurs to me that we could have

some fun "punking" future generations. All I'd need to do is ask for fans to carve the words "The End" and the date 12/21/3012 into rocks, walls and streets all around the world. Imagine the consternation in 1,000 years. Suck on that, Mayas.

Here is one of the more popular Maya-related images I shared:

MAYANS

Said the world would end in 2012

Didn't see the Spanish coming.

It wasn't more than a few minutes after posting this that I was treated to a quick history lesson by my Facebook fans. "George, don't blame the Spanish for the decline of the Mayans! You're perpetuating anti-colonialism with false information!!!" I learned that my post was wrong on two counts. First, the Maya civilization had its height between 250 and 900 A.D., and then collapsed before 1000 A.D., long before the Spanish conquered the Yucatan Peninsula in the 1500s. Some speculate that it was overpopulation, others suggest a prolonged drought, or perhaps disease. We may never really know for sure, because one thing the Spanish *did* do was destroy all of the Maya texts that might have told us. Nice going. So while no one is quite sure what caused the decline of the Maya, it clearly wasn't the Spanish, who were pretty late to the party with their guns and smallpox (if you haven't read *Guns, Germs and Steel* by Jared Diamond, it's worth the time. Fascinating).

Second, though December 21, 2012 is the end of the so-called time cycle for the Maya, the Maya never predicted it as the actual end of the world, as many believe. Like an odometer, it simply meant their calendar would turn over to a new "13th" cycle around that date. As an interesting tidbit, the calendar left to us by the Romans was hardly a model of accuracy, as it had to be corrected by decree in 46 B.C. to account for inaccuracies in year lengths (that confusing year apparently went on for 445 days). So no one knows for certain if 12/21/12 in fact was to be the day the Maya calendar ran out.

Fans with very dark senses of humor pointed out that the death of a certain celebrity in 2012 did not bode well for humanity's chances.

Dick Clark 1929 - 2012

How can we possibly

ring in the new year?

Well played, Mayans. Well played.

© Christopher Dodge - Fotolia.com Used with permission.

A second popular indicator of the coming of the end was the pregnancy (and feared but unfounded due date) of a reality television star, whose popularity still perplexes me:

SNOOKIES DUE DATE
12/21/12

I admit, I had to look up who Snooki was when I saw this, and I still don't get it.

Fans were also quick to point out that Hostess Twinkies were supposed to survive even a nuclear holocaust, but went out of production just weeks before December 21, 2012. Again, well played, Maya.

I also blame "zombie-philia" in part for our collective end-of-the-world mania. I've found that people under 30, in particular, have a keen sense of the undead and how to deal with them in the event they rise:

Clueless about his life... but has a full survival plan for the Zombie apocalypse.

In 2012, zombies leapt off the big screen and into the headlines with news reports of a homeless man who had his face chewed off by another man — truly the stuff of horror films. Rumor was that the assailant had been hallucinating on some kind of drug, dubbed on the street as "bath salts," but this was never corroborated. Nevertheless, the zombie apocalypsados pounced on the news as evidence of the "impending ending."

Right on cue, memes sprung up all over the Internet. My personal favorite poked fun at Carly Rae Jepsen's cloying "Call Me Maybe" song that seemed to be everywhere:

A popular related meme had Yoda singing this song, in his signature syntax. "Met you I just did, hmm? Call me you will maybe, hmm?" It goes to show, you can't go wrong with a Yoda post.

During that week, everywhere I looked on the Internet, there were zombie doom references. Fans compiled news stories from around the country that they swore corroborated that flesh-eating creatures were rampant. Mom chews off husband's penis. Boy bites off own arm. Man chops up roommate, stores in fridge to eat later. My own Facebook wall was full with fan images of zombie inspired attacks: peanut people devouring one another, stick figures dismembering their own, even gentle garden gnomes zombified into a rampaging pack of the undead.

There's something about zombies that fascinates us beyond what the movies have shown, a morbid fascination with, well, the morbid.

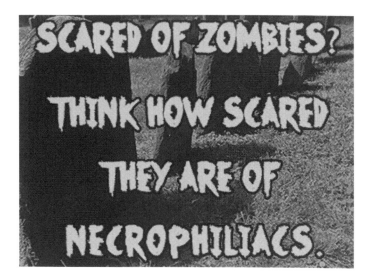

Gross indeed. Other popular 2012 predictions include disturbances within the heavens, everything from unprecedented planetary alignments to massive solar flares destroying our little blue home. Cults predicted the coming of aliens to destroy us, or of the true Second Coming. I began to wonder, what accounts for our collective affinity for the apocalypse? What is it about "the end" that makes it always seem just around the corner? And why do lawns in post-apocalyptic always appear freshly mowed if there's no one around to do it but the zombies?

It's one of the few areas in which science and many religions come to the same basic conclusion: We're doomed. The end is heralded in fire and brimstone, whether it's the return of the Savior or our sun going supernova in a few billion more years. Man can hasten The End of Days, whether through terrible wars, catastrophic damage to our environment, or even playing at God. Indeed, even some in the scientific world were unnerved at the news that CERN (the European Organization for Nuclear Research) would attempt collision of particles at near light speed, all in service of the search for the subatomic particle known as Higgs boson, which the press dismayingly has dubbed the "God Particle."

A Higgs boson particle walks into a church.

The priest asks, "What are you doing here?"

"What do you mean?" the particle says, "You can't have mass without me."

© valdis torms - Fotolia.com. Used with Permission

Here's another favorite:

© perfectmatch - Fotolia.com. Used with Permission

Our musings about our own destruction in some ways marks us as self-aware and separates us from other species on Earth. Our own attempts to defy our own temporal and physical limitations provide ample fodder for apocalypse watchers.

Many point to humankind's bold but, some caution, foolhardy attempt to unlock the secrets of the physical and natural world, unleashing devastation and misery instead of enlightenment. The atom bomb, a man-made super virus run amok, robot armies taking control — all are cautionary tales, where our technology vastly exceeds our collective social wisdom, allowing our discoveries to turn upon and destroy us. It is the ultimate evolutionary irony that our own over-developed brains may be our undoing. Perhaps it is no secret, then, that it is the brain that zombies find so delectable.

Perhaps our obsession with the apocalypse stems from the now irrefutable evidence that It. Has. Happened. Before. The sudden disappearance of the mighty dinosaurs, many posit from a huge meteor strike, is now part of our common understanding, affecting our own sense of vulnerability.

In late 2012, Apophis, an asteroid the size of two football fields, was predicted by astronomers to travel fairly close to the Earth. There is a chance, however small, that it could be deflected just enough by our own gravity to come zipping back to smack straight into us, some predict in 2036. Now, that probably won't happen, but the point is, for the first time we are keenly aware of celestial doomsday rocks and how close they will visit. Our delectable brains get fired up about it, and Morgan Freeman has to save the Earth again.

What is clear to astronomers and doomsday predictors alike is that we do have to figure a way off this planet, for one day the party will end. Happily for our species, it was never going to be 2012. We still get a very long time to figure out space travel, or come up with the antidote, or dig ourselves giant cities underground to protect against the radioactive clouds. I can't help but postulate that there is something oddly comforting in imagining an end we share together, rather than alone, and that this feeds our mutual obsession with Doomsday. The apocalypse that wipes out 99.99% of us doesn't discriminate by race, class, or geography. As it turns out, everyone's brains do in fact taste the same.

Getting My Facefix

Over the past year and a half, I've come to develop a unique bond not only with Facebook, but with some of the folks who work there. As an avid user with a fan base populated by many nerds and geeks, perhaps it shouldn't have come as a surprise to me that techies who work at Facebook actually follow my page and, as a consequence, might prove responsive to my concerns. In fact, I recall reading an article that claimed my page is more heavily trafficked by Facebook employees than Mark Zuckerberg's page (sorry, Mark, if that's true).

I first began a direct line of communication with "Facebook Engineering" in early 2012. At the time, I had been noticing that some of my posts seemed to "disappear" after I posted them, only to reappear minutes or even half an hour later, as if emerging from a wormhole. I was never sure whether the picture was truly "back" — i.e. actually appearing on fans' newsfeeds — or whether it was simply appearing on my wall and not anywhere else.

The same thing was happening to certain fan posts. Many fans would attempt, as I did when my own post failed to upload properly, to repost the image. And repost. And repost. This had the effect, after some time, of generating multiple copies of the same image on my wall, like so many movie posters on a construction site barrier. In my own case, images often would all upload at once but appear as an "album" rather than individual pictures. (Here's a Facebook tip: If you want people to actually see your photos, don't upload them all at once as an album. Upload them one by one, preferably more than two hours apart, otherwise Facebook may lump them together, and nobody will bother to flip through the album. Think about it — don't you brace yourself when someone sits you down on a couch to flip through their "album" of pictures?)

It was even more unfortunate when fans concluded that their posted images or links had disappeared because I had deleted them, as if I somehow was offended that they had used my wall to promote their cause. I would receive many of these types of angry wall posts after people went back to my wall to review their posts:

> *"GEORGE, I'M SORRY THAT YOU TOOK OFFENSE AT MY ATTEMPT TO BRING YOUR ATTENTION TO THE PLIGHT OF CHILDREN WITH MS. I WOULD HAVE THOUGHT A MAN OF YOUR STATURE WHO CLAIMS TO BE COMPASSIONATE WOULD NOT HAVE SO COLDLY DELETED MY MESSAGE OF HOPE. UNFRIEND."*

Good heavens, what a mess. I made a sincere effort to respond to each of these and explain that I never delete fan posts unless they contain hate speech or are obviously spam, that Facebook probably had swallowed up their posts temporarily, and they should be patient. But this happened so often that it became impossible for me to respond to each distraught fan, and so I endured post after tearful post from disenchanted fans.

The problem became acute enough that I actively had to monitor how my own posts were faring to determine whether there was an issue with any given one. In a particularly troubling week, it seemed every post I made failed to make it on to anyone's newsfeed. I could tell something was wrong because the number of likes and shares would mysteriously drop to negligible numbers, or simply stop rising altogether — meaning they had vanished off of everyone's feeds. Brad, of course, thought I was being paranoid, but the numbers spoke for themselves.

So I did what any customer would do. I complained.

"Fans," I asked, "Facebook appears to be acting up today. Could you do me a favor and visit my wall, and let me know whether you saw my two posts from earlier today?"

Hundreds of fans responded that they indeed had not seen my posts. Many assumed I had taken a mysterious hiatus from my daily Facefix. Others asked how they could ensure that they saw all my posts (there is no real way to ensure this, as I explain in a later chapter). After I posted my alert, imagine my surprise when I received wall posts from members of the Facebook Engineering team, alerting me, in turn, that they were investigating the issue. The nerd in me thrilled. One engineer, Mark Callaghan, blogged about the experience:

> *GEORGE TAKEI HAS A LOT OF FANS WITH US AND SINCE WE'VE ALL LIKED HIS PAGE, A WHILE BACK SOME OF US SAW AN UPDATE FROM HIM ABOUT AN INCONSISTENCY IN HIS FACEBOOK EXPERIENCE. WE REALIZED WHAT HE WAS EXPERIENCING WAS AN ISSUE WE WERE ALREADY TRYING TO FIX ON THE DATABASE SIDE, SO WHEN WE SAW HIM POST, IT GAVE US MORE INFORMATION THAT HELPED US GET CLOSER TO RESOLVING THE ISSUE. THIS ALLOWED US TO IMPROVE HIS EXPERIENCE, AND IN TURN, THE EXPERIENCE OF EVERYONE ELSE ON FACEBOOK.*

In "tech speak," on his blog, Callaghan was providing technical insight into challenges of scalability with MySQL on Facebook's multi-core servers. Truthfully, I don't understand this, but in plain English, it would appear my post had assisted their team with some real world troubleshooting.

Reading this, I suddenly realized what Dorothy must have felt like when meeting The Wizard. These are the live folks behind what happens on Facebook! I had peeked behind the curtain.

At times, I've come to the defense of Facebook, as when it rolled out its new Timeline user interface. The Internet was so abuzz with dire warnings and predictions, one would think a cataclysmic event had occurred, rather than an honest attempt to improve the product. So I did what came naturally: I spoofed it in a brief video. In it, I advised that the future of humanity was not threatened by the Timeline change itself, but by the possibility that one could go back in time to change one's status. Metaphysical purists no doubt will point out here that the concept of backward time travel is theoretically problematic because of the temporal paradox, but that's another book, probably in another parallel lifetime. In my spoof video I had a great deal of fun imagining what my own Timeline would look like in the year 2293, with the help of some creative staff members. I'm sure it did little to quell rumors of a feud between Bill Shatner and myself.

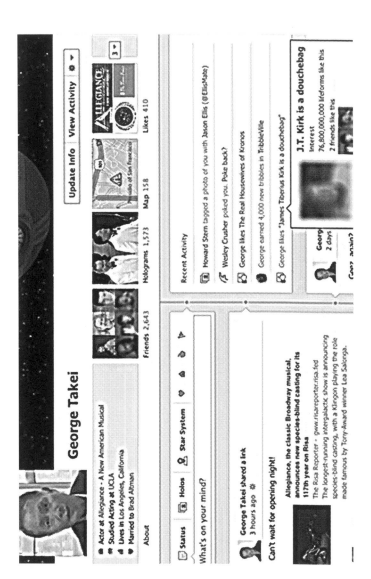

George Takei

Update Info | View Activity | ⚙ ▼

About

⚙ Actor at Allegiance - A New American Musical
⚙ Studied Acting at UCLA
◀ Lives in Los Angeles, California
♥ Married to Brad Altman

Friends 2,643   Holograms 1,573   Map 158   Likes 410

📄 Status   🖼 Holos   ☄ Star System   ◈ ◈ ◈ ▲

What's on your mind?

George Takei shared a link
3 hours ago ⚙

Can't wait for opening night!

Allegiance, the classic Broadway musical, announces new species-blind casting for its 117th year on Risa

The Risa Reporter - www.risareporter.risa.fed
The longest-running intergalactic show is announcing species-blind casting, with a Klingon playing the role made famous by Tony-Award winner Lea Salonga.

Recent Activity

📷 Howard Stern tagged a photo of you with Jason Ellis (@EllisMate)

🖋 Wesley Crusher poked you. Poke back?

🖼 George likes The Real Housewives of Kronos

● George earned 4,000 new tribbles in TribbleVille

🖼 George likes "James Tiberius Kirk is a douchebag"

J.T. Kirk is a douchebag

Interest
76,800,000,000 lifeforms like this
2 friends like this

George
2 days

Now, on the flip side, I haven't always been a complete fan of what Facebook is up to. In June of 2012, I saw an advertisement for "promoted posts" and read some articles about how Facebook was planning to make more money by implementing them. Promoted posts, as I understand them, are a way to charge pages and brands to reach more of their fans. This alarmed me, because I wasn't sure I would be able to maintain the engagement with my fans. I posted this on my page:

> "**FB** USED TO ALLOW FANS TO ELECT TO SEE **ALL** POSTS BY SELECTING 'ALL UPDATES' FROM THE RIGHT HAND CORNER OF A POST. **FOR** COMMUNITY PAGES SUCH AS THIS, THOUGH, **FB** RECENTLY DECIDED THAT ONLY CERTAIN FANS WILL SEE CERTAIN POSTS, AND IT PLANS TO ASK ME TO PAY FOR MORE FAN VIEWS.
>
> **I** UNDERSTAND THAT **FB** HAS TO MAKE MONEY, ESPECIALLY NOW THAT IT IS PUBLIC, BUT IN MY VIEW THIS DEVELOPMENT TURNS THE NOTION OF 'FANS' ON ITS HEAD."

My general concern was that the wonderful, freewheeling marketplace of ideas was about to be gobbled up by the companies most able to pay to have their messages delivered. I certainly would not be able to fork out thousands of dollars per update to ensure my fans saw something I'd shared.

My frustrations did not go unnoticed. Another engineer at Facebook, Phil Zigoris, responded quickly, respectfully assuring me as follows:

TO THE ESTEEMED MR. GEORGE TAKEI, I SAW YOUR POST EARLIER (AT THE TOP OF MY FEED, IN FACT) ON SUPPOSED CHANGES TO THE WAY YOUR POSTS WERE DELIVERED TO FANS. I WORK AT FB AND EVEN WORK ON THE PRODUCT YOU DESCRIBE, AND I WANTED TO DROP A NOTE TO SAY THAT WE'VE CHANGED NOTHING ABOUT THE WAY PAGE POSTS ARE DELIVERED TO FANS. I STILL SEE YOUR POSTS IN MY FEED ALL THE TIME (KEEP 'EM COMING). THE MAIN POINT OF CONFUSION WE'VE SEEN IS THAT PAGES DON'T REALIZE THAT THEIR POSTS WERE NEVER REACHING 100% OF FANS. IF YOU GO TO YOUR PAGE INSIGHTS, YOU'LL SEE THIS HAS ALWAYS BEEN THE CASE.

AND IT MAKES SENSE IF YOU STOP AND THINK ABOUT IT: THERE IS JUST NO WAY TO SEE ALL OF THE STUFF HAPPENING ON FB IN YOUR FEED. PERSONALLY, I HAVE OVER 700 FRIENDS AND HAVE PROBABLY FANNED 1000S OF PAGES, THERE IS NO WAY I CAN SEE ALL OF THEIR POSTS IN MY FEED EVERYDAY. FORTUNATELY, FB DOES A PRETTY GOOD JOB RANKING CONTENT BASED ON THE PEOPLE AND PAGES I INTERACT WITH THE MOST. SO NATURALLY, GEORGE TAKEI AND TACO BELL ARE USUALLY AT THE TOP OF MY FEED.

ALL PROMOTED PAGE POSTS DOES IS OFFER AN EASY WAY FOR PAGE ADMINS TO PAY TO PROMOTE A POST USING FB ADS USING FUNCTIONALITY THAT ALREADY EXISTED. A LOT OF BUSINESSES USE POSTS TO PROMOTE SALES, CONCERTS, ETC AND ITS AN EASY WAY TO GET MORE DISTRIBUTION AND WE'VE GOTTEN A LOT OF POSITIVE FEEDBACK FROM PAGES ABOUT THE PRODUCT.

While this addressed some of my technical ignorance, it left open the question of whether money was going to tip the balance in favor of big corporations when it came to Facebook "real estate."

The question was ripe enough for even *The Wall Street Journal* to take interest. A reporter called and interviewed me about my thoughts on the matter.

Here is an excerpt from that interview:

WSJ: *Are you frustrated by this news?*

MR. TAKEI: I am still learning how Facebook works and trying hard to keep up with its many changes. And I understand that Facebook has to make money. But what is frustrating is that this offer comes during a time when I saw my general reach (43 million per week) inexplicably dropping by 25% down to 34 million, even as the number of people talking about the page was rising (to now over 2.5 million per week) and the number of fans was growing at around 7,000 per day.

I asked myself, is Facebook doing something to shrink my fan reach, at the same time it is telling me to pay to reach more of them? So yes, it was frustrating to feel pressure to pay to reach fans.

WSJ: *Any plans to pay Facebook so more fans can see your posts?*

MR. TAKEI: I don't currently have any such plans. Nearly all of my posts are just things I find funny, or touching, or thought-provoking. They have little to do with me personally, so I can't see myself paying extra for those.

WSJ: *Will this have any impact on your Facebook presence?*

MR. TAKEI: Fans are going to have to become educated on how the content they believe they have signed up for is actually handled, and at times take proactive measures to make sure their "news feed" contains what they want it to contain. For my part, I am getting a crash course in what content makes its way into what stream, and why. I know that to stay relevant in social media, you can't go radio silent for weeks on vacation and expect the world not to have changed. At least, certainly not on Facebook.

Despite my initial concerns, the algorithm Facebook is using to determine post placement has caused my page to come out fine. Facebook continues to search for a way to satisfy its investors while maintaining the integrity and core of its free user engagement, a delicate balance that always threatens to set users on edge, myself included. We have become accustomed to this "free" service provided, and are quick to balk at any hint of commercialism, which of course makes no sense when you consider that Facebook ultimately must make gobs of money to justify its stock price. Well, perhaps not gobs any longer given its current stock price, but you get my drift.

After one more recent incident, Facebook Engineering extended an open invitation for me to ask them direct questions rather than post about them on my wall. This happened after I shared a concern that a French newspaper had reported. The rumor was that Facebook had published, in error, its users' private messages as "wall posts" in the Timeline before the year 2009. This rumor spread rather quickly, in part because wall posts from that era did in fact more closely resemble what today's more savvy users would identify as private messaging (in fact, private messaging wasn't even available on Facebook back then). I shared this concern with my fans, but within minutes received contrary information from

Facebook Engineering. I decided then to take down the post and investigate the claim more thoroughly.

I am still getting used to the idea that, because my posts reach so many fans so quickly, I have a higher responsibility to ensure that they are accurate, lest I become part of the reason a false rumor spreads. Whether I should be held to a higher standard is still an open question, as I'm neither a journalist nor an expert, but I do understand that sheer numbers have begun to make the question moot. Knowing that I can have a back channel to Facebook, if needed, is an unexpected honor, and I plan to take advantage of it when confronted again with technical questions.

Indeed, Facebook recently extended an invitation to me personally to come visit their headquarters, and I hope to be able to take them up on the offer if I can find a window when I will be in the San Francisco Bay Area. I don't want to get too cozy with the company, mind you, as I'm still just a user and have my share of issues.

In the next chapter, I discuss some of the specifics about Facebook and its algorithms. It's a bit on the technical side, but a lot of folks who use social media regularly wanted me to spill some secrets of my success on Facebook.

I have a great deal of respect for what is still a fledgling company, for despite its detractors Facebook has managed to connect over a billion people and certainly has changed my life in myriad unexpected and positive ways.

And let's face it, we all still need our Facefix.

I'm on the Edge

Fans (and the press) often wonder how a 75-year old actor who had his heyday in a science fiction series from the 1960s came to have some three million fans on Facebook. I honestly often wonder the same thing. Looking back, there are a few reasons that come to mind, none of which I understood when I first started sharing online. It turns out, the success of my page is mostly tied up in something Facebook calls "EdgeRank."

I should preface this by saying I am not certain exactly how "EdgeRank" works. It's a secret algorithm that Facebook guards closely. But I do understand some of its basic principles, and how they worked to my page's advantage in the early going. So nerd out with me a bit in this chapter, and I'll let you in on some secrets on why I think my page got the "edge" when it comes to fans and fan interaction, and why I worry that Facebook actually might be pushing some of its users to the edge.

Before I jump in, let me preface this by explaining that I have been both a champion and critic of Facebook, but always with the hope of creating a better experience for everyone. Admittedly, it took me some time to come up to speed on how Facebook works, and to pinpoint where it works best, and where it sometimes falls short. Lately, my status updates or even my comments on other pages about Facebook's ranking algorithm have gotten picked up by the press, especially after Facebook's less-than-optimal initial public offering. Everyone is wondering whether Facebook is on the right track, and as an avid user with one of the most engaged fan bases, I've become something of a magnet for controversy.

Some basic concepts first. Contrary to what many users believe, when you post something on Facebook, it doesn't show up in all of your friends' newsfeeds. Just imagine if it did; basic math dictates this would soon overload the system. So instead, Facebook assigns an "EdgeRank" to each post to determine whether it will appear in someone else's feed. If people frequently comment, share or click "like" on your posts, it's more likely that your future posts will appear in their newsfeeds.

This gives a distinct advantage to those who got in the game early and drew attention, because their posts will tend to edge out other posts. Consider this: If there's limited real estate (i.e., what can physically appear in your newsfeed), and Facebook gives greater priority to the posts of those you've interacted with before, then the chance that you'll see a new friend's or page's post is comparatively lower. Conversely, think of all those annoying people you don't really know that well yet are constantly liking or commenting on your status updates; your posts wind up on their newsfeeds more frequently than on the streams of your good friends, who are likely largely ignoring your posts because, well, they're your good friends already and don't need to read your statuses.

This aspect of EdgeRank can be distressing for community, celebrity and company pages that want to promote on Facebook. They discover, for example, that their attempts to reach their fans — even those that have clicked "like" on their pages — often fall short because there simply isn't much existing engagement with them. This means that their posts, however well-crafted, often never even reach much of their intended audience. One article I read suggested that the average post by a page only reaches about

16% of its fans due to EdgeRank and the fact that, shockingly, people are not on Facebook 24/7. This presents a bit of a conundrum, because in order to gain engagement, pages need to reach their fans, but they can't reach their fans without first gaining more engagement.

In mid-2012, Facebook put forth a solution: Promoted Posts. Under this program, pages can pay to ensure that their posts reach more of their fans. It has been popular of late to lay into Facebook over Promoted Posts, which some say reduces the visibility of non-profit, community or small business sites in favor of larger corporations willing to spend serious money. Page administrators cry foul for a few reasons.

First, many point out that Facebook encourages pages to use advertising to grow the number of fans, but never did a great job explaining that most of those people would not wind up seeing the very pages they signed up for — unless they stayed engaged. In other words, people spent money — sometimes considerable amounts — to grow a base that now may be out of reach in most cases, unless they pay more.

© Eléonore H - Fotolia.com.
Used with permission

Second, many comparatively large pages with a wide reach really can't afford to pay thousands of dollars per post to reach more fans. I would never really consider spending money to reach my fans because, frankly, I'm not in it for the same reasons as Coca-Cola or Starbucks. As I write this, I'm looking at my most recent post, which Facebook says I can pay $4,000 to have reach over a million people. This is ironic to me, because it already reached over a million. So what exactly would I be buying? It's not really that clear.

Finally, Facebook indicates with Promoted Posts that fans will be told they are being promoted to because the post will appear as a "sponsored story" much the same way certain establishments appear in sites such as Yelp. But fans view any kind of sponsored or commercial post with suspicion. I know this first hand: Anytime I try to sell anything online, including the book you are now reading, fans know and take a more jaundiced view of the effort. It's simply part of human nature, especially when very few of my other posts ask anything of the fans.

I don't begrudge Facebook for wanting to make more money. They're now a publicly traded company, and they have to answer to different masters than before. But Facebook should tread carefully before this becomes a huge PR problem. As pages have seen their numbers crash, many have threatened to leave Facebook in search of cheaper ways to reach fans, such as Twitter or even Google+. Or they'll stop spending money trying to acquire fans, knowing that they have to spend money again just to reach them.

When I asked other Page owners to convey their experiences with Facebook and its EdgeRank system, I received back almost universally negative comments. Here are a handful of examples out of dozens and dozens of complaints people left in responses to my inquiry:

> *I AM A STAY AT HOME MOM WHO HAS WORKED TIRELESSLY IN THE LAST YEAR AND A HALF TO BUILD [MY JEWELRY BUSINESS.] I HAVE 8,300 FANS, AND NOW ONLY A FRACTION OF THEM SEE MY POSTS, EVEN WHEN I PAY. IT HAS SEVERELY AFFECTED MY BUSINESS.*

I WOULD LIKEN THIS TO EXTORTION. "HEY, HERE'S TRAFFIC, BUT NOW WE'RE GOING TO TAKE IT AWAY FROM YOU AND MAKE YOU PAY FOR IT."

AS SOMEONE WHO RUNS A FACEBOOK PAGE, I'M DISAPPOINTED THAT ANYONE WHO CHOOSES TO FOLLOW OUR PAGE HAS TO OPT-IN AFTER "LIKING" US TO HAVE OUR POSTS SHOW UP ON THEIR PAGE, ESPECIALLY SINCE THAT INFO ISN'T EXPLICITLY INCLUDED ANYWHERE.

I RUN A PAGE DESIGNED TO PROMOTE AWARENESS FOR EPILEPSY. HIT RATE HAS DROPPED. MEANWHILE, SHELL ADS (AS IN THE GAS COMPANY) KEEP APPEARING ON MY PERSONAL TIMELINE. TO SAY I'M PISSED ABOUT IT IS AN UNDERSTATEMENT.

TRAFFIC DROPPED A TON, THEN WE CHUCKED $15 DOLLARS INTO PROMOTING AND IT WENT UP BRIEFLY - I TOOK ADVANTAGE OF THIS BY LEARNING HOW TO INCREASE TRAFFIC (OURS IS DOG RESCUE AND WE ARE DEPENDENT ON BEING SEEN) AND IT WORKED FOR AWHILE AND THEN BAM! -TRAFFIC PLUMMETED EVEN LOWER THAN BEFORE. IT IS FRUSTRATING AND EXHAUSTING TRYING TO KEEP UP WITH THE BEST WAYS TO THWART THE FACEBOOK TRICKS.

I MANAGE A NOT-FOR-PROFIT ARTS PAGE AND WE'VE SEEN DRASTIC REDUCTIONS ON OUR NUMBERS. I THINK THE ANNOYANCE IS THAT WHEN YOU 'LIKE' A PAGE IT'S BECAUSE YOU WANT TO SEE THE CONTENT. PERHAPS, FACEBOOK NEEDS TO DEVELOP A 'KINDA LIKE' BUTTON. ASKING FANS TO GO BACK AND CHANGE ALL THEIR SETTINGS IS RIDICULOUS.

My own page saw some fairly drastic and worrisome collapses in reach and engagement during July and September of 2012. It was frustrating for me because this drop came at the same time Facebook launched its Promoted Pages campaign, leading me to believe that the two were connected, and that I was under pressure to pay to keep my reach up. Facebook explained that the two had nothing to do with each other, and that changes were all intended to improve user experience.

The problem of course is that as more and more real estate in the Newsfeed is purchased by companies that can afford to advertise and buy that space, fewer people will see posts from pages that they actually have liked. In order to prevent a slide in engagement, I have taken some proactive measures.

First, I remind fans periodically that the more engaged they are, the more likely I will appear in their feeds. Second, I asked fans to add me to their "interests" so that they can view my post together with other interests at their leisure. And third, I lately have begun telling fans to "Get Notifications" of my posts, so that they receive an alert that I posted and then can go to my page for the latest. The last option appears to have made some real difference in my engagement numbers, because people are not limited to being online exactly when my post would cross their feed — they can go back and look on their own time later.

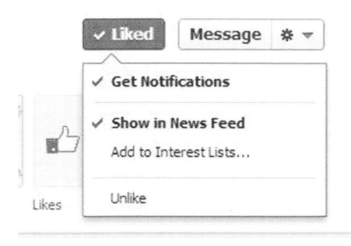

In November of 2012, just days before this book went to print, Facebook rolled out a new feature called "Pages Feed" which users could select. The idea behind Pages feed is that users who want to see more of their "liked" pages' posts could filter their feed so that only posts from pages (and not friends) appeared in their feed. This is a welcome development which goes some way towards answering the critics. But for folks who have "liked" many pages, this will probably do little to increase the visibility of small pages. Nor is it yet clear whether people will enable this filter on a regular basis. Still, it is great to see Facebook responding to user feedback. Some press stories credit my vocal criticism of Facebook's Newsfeed for this new feature, but I imagine it was in the works long before I even raised the issue publicly.

Because my posts already reach a relatively high percentage of my fans, who share it with their networks whenever they interact with me, I'm admittedly something of an unlikely critic of Facebook's EdgeRank algorithm. But let me be clear: I am concerned primarily with transparency, not with the actual algorithm itself, which appears to do its job. I personally can't think of any better way for Facebook to assign relevance to posts and determine who should see them.

This doesn't mean, however, that the solution is something like Promoted Pages. If Facebook intends to keep the program, it needs to be completely upfront with page owners about how few of their fans actually see each post now and what they can expect after they pay for a post. For example, if EdgeRank rewards interactivity, pages might want to limit their promoted posts to those that could go highly viral but need an extra push. Page owners thus need to educate themselves about how Facebook works, especially before spending a lot of money on Promoted Posts.

My outspokenness about Facebook and willingness to voice my concerns has gotten me into some hot water. For example, I was accused flat out by prominent technology blogger Robert Scoble of whining that I want *all* my posts seen by *all* my fans. This simply isn't true. I know that such a demand is both impractical and rather greedy given the limited space on each user's feed. Scoble also accused me of creating so much Internet "noise" with my posting that I ought to "sit down and shut up." Well, I didn't become an advocate for equality and civil rights by sitting down and shutting up, so I was not about to do that. Scoble even admitted in his tirade that, though he hates my posts, his wife enjoys them and shares them with him all the time. I put out this cheeky tweet in response:

George Takei @GeorgeTakei   10 Nov
Scoble says my content is "noise"--but his wife's a fan. Well, when one man's post gets another man's wife going...
scobleizer.com/2012/11/09/the...
Collapse   ← Reply   ⇄ Retweet   ★ Favorite

All kidding aside, Scoble does miss a basic point. His wife and other fans actively have decided that they want to see my content. They want to hear my noise — and probably don't consider it "noise" at all. They clicked "like" on my page with the expectation that they would see my posts, or at least most of them. Many are surprised to learn that they receive only a fraction of them. If Scoble prefers not to have me take up space on his newsfeed from his wife's shares, he should speak to her and tell her to screen him, rather than call on me to self-censor.

I do occasionally look at the "insights" for interactivity provided by Facebook. If I've understood them correctly, my "reach" (meaning, the number of people who have seen a given post) averages between 1 and 2 million. Because at the time I'm typing this I've got about three million fans, that means a reach of between 33 and 66 percent per post, versus the standard 15-16 percent.

I have also noticed that more pages than ever have started including a "call to action" with their posts that asks users to click "like" and "share." This is online marketing 101. Traditional wisdom dictates that getting people to take any kind of action is important (after all, it increases the EdgeRank your future posts have with them). A simple "ask" often does the trick. When I've put a call to action in my posts, the response rate often doubles or triples.

But I caution that asks should be used sparingly. People don't like to be treated as mere clicks or numbers, or bluntly told what to do. My own fan base sometimes tsk-tsks me for such posts, and I admit it does feel somehow forced if it happens too frequently. The act of liking or sharing should feel like a voluntary gesture, not a favor or compelled response. And as more pages figure out the short-term advantage of asks, Facebook has started to feel overburdened with these types of demands. Click "like" if you want this sick dog to find a happy home, keep scrolling if you don't care! Click "share" if you feel the love of Jesus!

Lately I've been trying not too often to add to the "ask" pollution, and I'd prefer it if I only had to include a call to action when it makes sense. But because of the way EdgeRank works, it's nearly impossible to ignore the power of the "ask." So to make things more palatable, I often enjoy presenting games, such as a popular song with lyrics in "Spockese" with instructions to "like" and "share" when you "get it."

> *WE ONLY ARE RECENTLY ACQUAINTED, AND THIS MAY SEEM HIGHLY ILLOGICAL, BUT HERE IS A NUMERICAL SEQUENCE BY WHICH YOU MAY CONTACT ME VIA YOUR COMMUNICATION DEVICE, PERHAPS YOU WILL MAKE USE OF IT.*

I also like to post puzzles to see if we can collectively solve them. This was one famous one:

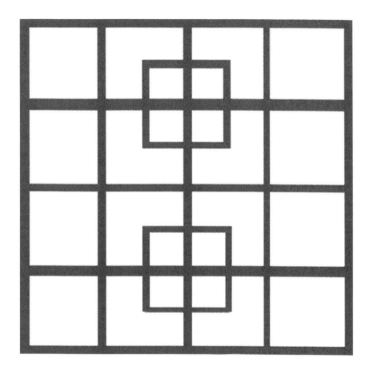

I asked the fans to post how many squares they could count and to share this with their friends. It turns out there are 40 — though I could only get up to 34 on my first attempt. When some fans began to post comments that they could count 40 squares, it encouraged the rest of us to go back and try harder.

I also enjoy caption contests. In the early days, I would simply post an image, invite captions, and attempt to read through the comments. But this soon proved impossible. For one caption contest, with an infamous image of my friend Nichelle Nichols (*Star*

Trek's Uhura) toying sexily with me on the bridge of the *Enterprise*, we received something like 13,000 comments with proposed captions. I had to divide the work among myself, Brad and our intern, and it took days to go through it all. The winning entry was Uhura declaring, "The captain kisses like a girl" and me as Sulu responding, "I know."

I've come to learn that, on Facebook, an image appears to get more traction than mere text. This is largely because an image takes up more space and is more attractive to the eye than text or a link. When scrolling through wall posts by fans, my own eye is drawn to images. I simply don't have enough time or patience to read all of the text-based posts others leave.

My own experiences led me to a strong preference for images over text. After months of posting plain status updates and links to articles, I happened to share a funny image that had a caption built into it. I don't remember what the image was exactly, but I do recall being surprised that it received many more likes and shares than my other posts did.

It dawned on me that this probably was the way to go if I wanted to engage more successfully with fans. From that point forward, I focused nearly exclusively on sharing funny, inspiring, or just plain random images. As a consequence, my Facebook page was one of the first to adopt a practice of "meme" sharing. As a rule these images also contained text; this way, whenever fans shared the photo with their friends, the humor associated with the original image would survive no matter what else the sharer added. Because, by accident and not by design, I always uploaded the meme myself rather than shared it from another page, this wound up inadvertently creating in each meme a viral advertisement for my page.

Images also have the plain advantage of being much more likely to be "shared" than mere text posts. Consider your own Facebooking: how often do you "share" the "status updates" of your friends? If you're feeling charitable, you may click "like" on them, and sometimes leave a comment. But when they post an image that has some general appeal, you are more likely to share that image and comment on it in your own way. Because sharing appears to have more weight in Facebook's ranking system than mere liking, images again appear to be a better bet.

On the other hand, when I have tried to promote something else on my Facebook page by creating a link out, Facebook appears to penalize that post with a lower EdgeRank. I noticed this particularly during my efforts to publicize the Hurricane Sandy relief effort, which was hosted on another site called indiegogo.com. I could see that every time I reposted the link to the fundraiser, the number of people who actually saw the post went down. This leads me to speculate that Facebook somehow tracks whether a post contains a link to another site outside of Facebook, and reduces the EdgeRank of any post that contains that link again. I don't have any hard facts to back that suspicion up, but I can't think of any other reason why my posts received comparatively fewer views with each successive attempt.

A third lesson about EdgeRank that I learned was that, to stay engaged with your fans, you have to post with some frequency. On average, I'll post four or fives times during the day, usually when I've got downtime during a shoot, rehearsals, or a show. That means I need to find (or if I'm too busy, more likely Brad or one of our interns needs to find) at least that many funny or interesting things to post about daily. It can be a tall order, but I have the advantage of having an amazing fan base that makes this job fairly easy and straightforward. Many fans send mail to my website with funny images attached, but more often than not I need only look at my own wall to see what others have shared. There will be dozens and dozens of hilarious posts from all over the world on all manner of topics. Often I'll receive many copies of the same image. If it's been a few hours since I last posted, I'll pick something that tickles my fancy. When I get a few hours of free time, I can even line up several posts to go out over the course of a day, spaced out using a social media organizer like Hootsuite or the Facebook "Pages" application on my iPhone.

I don't know if EdgeRank takes into account how often you post. But I've found that something posted more than an hour back is far less likely to appear in a friend's newsfeed than something posted seconds ago. I draw this conclusion empirically, because the numbers of likes and shares that occur with the first 15 minutes or so of a post vastly outweigh what happens later. So if a fan isn't logged on at the time of one of my posts, the chance that it lands in his or her newsfeed diminishes quickly over time.

Some pages try to solve this problem by posting more frequently. This presents the very real risk of overposting. We all know friends who seem to post every half hour or more, and our eyes become trained to largely ignore the chatter. If we interacted with each post, it would eat up our whole day. I like to think of each of us as having a limited amount of interactive Facebook goodwill, which can be taxed if drawn upon with too much frequency.

There is also a phenomenon I call update cannibalism. By this I mean that posts made too close together literally will eat from each other's likes, comments and shares. Fans already may have interacted with something I posted an hour earlier, and thus are likely less willing to interact with my next post, even if it is funny or worthy in its own right. Fans also generally understand that everyone else can see much of their activity on Facebook, and no one wants to appear obsessed with a page like some kind of crazy virtual cheerleader.

Finally, it's important to consider the time of day you are posting, and to understand where your fans are and how they get their Facebook fixes. Although I have fans all over the world, many are largely concentrated on the two coasts of the U.S. I work in all kinds of different locations and hold down a very odd schedule, so I often begin posting as early as 6:30 a.m. in California, three hours behind the East Coast where folks are already at work. It turns out, many of my fans tend to check Facebook while at work on break (or even not on break), and in the evenings while at home on their computers or in front of the TV. Mid-week posts are some of my most viewed, while weekends are less busy. In fact, on weekends I suspect many fans may check Facebook using their phones while they are out running errands or enjoying the day. This used to result in fewer "shares" because the Facebook application on mobile devices didn't have a share option yet. This always baffled me, so I was pleased as punch to learn that Facebook at last had rolled out a "share" button on the mobile site. I expect this will help a great deal with engagement from my more mobile-phone obsessed fans.

Keep in mind that during certain peak hours, a lot of other people and pages are also posting on Facebook. This means more competition for the same number of spots, and thus a lower likelihood that a post will make it onto a friend's or fan's newsfeed. Indeed, if you have a lower interaction rate than other friends or pages that are posting at the same time, your post won't get seen — it will be edged out.

"But, George!" you might wonder. "Aren't you worried that giving away these secrets will give other pages the same edge you've had?" Not really, and it doesn't matter much to me anyway. I'm not out to have tens of millions of fans like Lady Gaga or President Obama; I'd rather have fans who truly interact with my page. It pleases me more that, as I write this, over three million people on my page are "talking about this" — meaning that many people joined, clicked like, shared or commented on something on my page in the past week. The three principles I've employed — past interactivity, a preference for images, and frequency of posting — have operated to propel my page forward and will probably keep it vibrant and growing, so long as fans continue actively to engage my posts, and so long as I keep putting shareable content out there. I don't intend to stop any time soon.

Oн Myyy!

George Fakei

At some point in my Internet life, I had sufficient clout (or Klout, as it were) to merit impostors. One in particular has continued to dog me throughout my time on Facebook. His screen name is George Takie, or sometimes George Tekai. I call him George Fakei. He uses my likeness and posts in my comment streams to appear as me, offering "free iPads" to anyone who clicks "like" on his page. I'm sure it's some kind of phishing scam or identity theft racket, and I've warned the users about it many times. In fact, I've had to say outright that I do not use <3 <3 <3 symbols to get anyone's attention, and I never type in ALL CAPS. But no matter how frequently I warn people, some still fall for the ruse.

> **Deb Jamerson** TOO FUNNY Love it!!!!!!!!! ×
> 38 minutes ago · Like
>
> **Vicki Wilson** So cute! What a crack-up
> 24 minutes ago · Like
>
> **Patricia Cassera** Too cute!
> 18 minutes ago · Like
>
> **George Takie** 💙 💙 click LIKE to get a free iPad! Only 15 left!
> a few seconds ago · Like

I don't know why anyone falls for George Fakei at all. Who on earth believes that I am giving out free Apple products? I haven't even bought an iPhone 5 yet (and am reluctant to, until they fix their maps).

Fans who see and recognize the impostor tend to do one of a few things. The more helpful ones will immediately block and report the post or comment to Facebook, sparing the rest of the fan base the need to even see it. Community vigilance, I've found, is the best solution. With hundreds of thousands of fans on the lookout, it is rare that any one pesky spammer will last for long. Once reported, the spam appears in the comment stream as a set of ellipses. But alas, even if he is banned from my page, George Fakei apparently simply creates another user profile with the same name and image, presumably with a different email, and returns the next day or even within hours on the next wall post to annoy the base and ensnare the unwitting.

Other fans will post a note on my wall or a comment in the stream alerting me to the scammer, on the assumption that I wasn't aware of him. The notes usually go something like this: "George, in case you didn't know, there is an impostor offering free iPhones who is using your name and image." This isn't very helpful, but it is well intentioned. Some fans will even post a link to the offending page, though this often results in other fans clicking on it and becoming victims. A few fans even have railed at me for "tricking" them into giving out personal information, not understanding that the spammer and I have no connection. I really don't know what to do about such folks except to sigh and explain the concept of the spammer to them.

Lastly, several fans a day will comment that I need to "change my password" because I "have been hacked." This is, of course, not what has happened. All that the impostor has done is created a fake account using my likeness and something close to my name. But the world is so filled with security breaches and spammed emails that the first conclusion is often that a hacker has breached my security protocols. If that had really happened, I imagine a much worse result, such as pornography strewn on my wall.

Believe you me, I have done everything I can to be rid of the pest, including enlisting the assistance of

Facebook Engineering to ensure that at least my own name cannot be misused by an impostor. While Facebook agreed to prevent anyone from registering the name George Takei as a fan page, that doesn't stop this particular impostor from creating all variations of my name. Facebook even went so far as to limit his ability to post the same comment multiple times — at least to slow his spam down in the comments on my posts. But lately he gets around this by adding some gibberish at the end of each post to fool their filters. Like a pesky rodent that figures its way past every obstacle, it looks like George Fakei is here to stay.

Apart from the impostor, another common question I receive is this: "Is this the real George Takei or just a fan page?" I understand the impulse for fans to know whether they are getting the real goods or not, but I really don't know how to reassure people more than I already have. After all, if I simply write back saying, "Yes, it really is me," how is the person on the other end to know that it isn't still some impostor?

When I first started on Twitter, there was a battle brewing over whether it was really me. Apparently someone had registered my name in the past and impersonated me for some time, causing some fans to become excited and then drop off in disappointment after learning of the ruse. The only way I could think of to verify my own identity was to link to my Twitter page from my website at georgetakei.com. That was proof enough for some people, but others wanted what was called a "verified account" from Twitter. These accounts were reviewed by Twitter and confirmed as authentic, and I had to jump through several hoops to get a "verified badge" placed on my Twitter page.

On Facebook I often see people comment under my posts poo-pooing the notion that the page is really mine. "Idiots, don't you know that this isn't the real George Takei?! Get a clue!" Those comments always amuse me, because their authors have no more basis for their skepticism than other fans have for their belief.

But now I have a confession. What I realized after a few months on Facebook, once I had over 300,000 fans and lots of comments and posts to sift through, was that I needed to enlist some help. I keep a fairly busy schedule, and am in studio or on set a great deal. It isn't always possible for me to update my page regularly, and darned near impossible to get through all of the comments. I had to shut off messaging early on, as my inbox was always embarrassingly full, and I didn't want fans to think I would just let their messages pile up and go unanswered.

Thank goodness for the help I got. First was Brad, who dutifully goes through all the fan mail, sifting through posts and sending me information or forwarding funny images to me. Without him, it would be hard to keep up with all of the information and communication that running my Facebook page requires. Second, I owe a debt to social media management tools such as Hootsuite (which I used for some time), which enabled me to pre-set a post to go out when I knew I would be busy or traveling. For example, if there were three images I wanted to share over the course of a day, I could pre-load them even the night before, and they would upload later for me. It was a lot like having an automatic sprinkler system. Later, I could go back and read the comments and laugh together with Brad over dessert. Now the Facebook Pages app has this functionality, making life easier for us all.

But even with Brad and handy social media applications, it still wasn't enough as the fan base grew and grew. And so, I caved and hired an intern. And then another. For the sake of their privacy I won't name their names, but they are terrific.

I have come to rely heavily on the folks who run the *Allegiance* website, which also hosts my blog. The production team over there is always willing to help me out with a quick video, with editing, and with setting up special fan applications. A good example is my fan contests. Facebook rules don't permit me to host actual contests and offer actual prizes to fans, even if I'm just giving away autographed photos. So I've turned to my friends at *Allegiance*, who manage an extensive web site and have the resources to create and manage databases of fans for me. I am truly indebted to them for their help.

So yes, other than when George Fakei shows up, it really is me and it really is my page. And as it continues to grow, I'm sure I'm going to one day have to hire more people to help me manage it and handle all the fan input. I hope that doesn't change the fun and informal nature of my fan interactions.

Nothing is so disappointing as making something you love doing daily into some kind of corporate structure. If that ever happens, I'll probably hang up my Facebook smock and spend my remaining time more in the real world.

It's on the Net, It Must Be True

In the play *8* by Dustin Lance Black, I play Dr. William Tan, a staunchly conservative defense witness for the backers of traditional marriage. In my brief scene, I cite "the Internet" as my source for my "evidence" that same-sex marriage is harmful to families and children. This always gets a laugh, because we all know, or should know, that the Internet isn't a place where reliable information is to be found.

Or is it? Many people now turn to Wikipedia as the most dependable source of information, yet that site is dependent on crowdsourcing of facts (with a host of checks, of course). Any one with a mischievous bent can alter text and facts on Wikipedia, so at any given time you can't have complete assurance that you're reading the truth.

Then again, it's about as well as we're going to do. It's been demonstrated time and again that "group intelligence" is more likely to be accurate than single postulations or guesses. A famous experiment conducted by finance professor Jack Treynor at the University of Southern California had students guess how many jellybeans were in a jar. The group's average was 871, when in fact there were 850. Only one person out of 56 in the class had a closer guess (don't just take my word for it, look it up on the Internet). A similar phenomenon occurred when townsfolk tried to guess the weight of a cow at a state fair, according to anecdotal accounts. Many of the guesses were very, very far off the mark. But the average of the guesses (with a large enough sample) was closer to the true weight than any single guess. Which reminds of me a recent joke:

We're also seeing major news outlets go entirely online, including the recent announcement by *Newsweek* that it would cease its print publication. As more media organizations inevitably follow suit, we will face a day, not long from now, when all of our information comes from digital sources, meaning that rumors and untruths can spread even more quickly than before.

Ironically, then, we live in a world where, because of our connectivity, a falsehood can be spread far and wide in a matter of seconds, even while our ability to maintain collective intelligence is without parallel throughout all of human history. Governments, churches, and educational institutes, once the keepers of order and social enlightenment, are now scrambling to remain relevant as our collective consciousness and connectivity grows.

Everything I learned in four years of college...

...can now be found on Wikipedia.

Watchdogs of the Internet, to no one's surprise, have

211

also sprung up in droves. I call these folks "Doubters." They have come to play, at least in their own minds, a crucial role in verifying facts and debunking fiction. They are also some of the most annoying people around. Like Grammar Nazis are to the purity of the English language online, the Doubters are there at the ready to curb the excesses of the Internet, stopping rumors in their tracks and raining on our collective meme parades.

On occasion I've posted unlikely but hilarious images: a manta ray photo-bombing snorkelers; a picture of a Starbucks van, door open over half the logo, so that it simply reads "Sucks"; or a photo of the UK swimming champion Tom Daley, in a Speedo, with sponsor "British Gas" splashed across his rear-end.

Oh myyy.

These were all pictures sent to me by fans. I didn't take them myself, nor do I claim that the pictures are "real." I have no basis to make that claim, and, after all, I am posting it on the Internet. But no matter what the circumstance, several Doubters will invariably immediately comment with the words "Photoshop" or, more succinctly, "Shopped." Now, they also don't usually have a basis for this claim, such as a link to the actual picture or a helpful dissection of the photo. They merely want to wreck it for everybody else, to be the Debbie Downers of the Web. These are the same people, I imagine, who fail to give spoiler alerts in movie reviews, try to ruin magic tricks at birthday parties, or tell six year olds that there really isn't a Santa Claus. Unable to appreciate the true humor or wonder of a picture, they'd rather crush our dreams with a condescending "told you so" than laugh along with the rest of us.

None of the examples I gave above — the ray, the van, the ass — were actually faked in any way. But it didn't stop the Doubters from calling it like they thought they saw it. What I've never really understood is what difference it makes if an image in a joke is real or not, especially on the Net. Either way, it's funny — the only distinction is whether the unlikely moment actually occurred, or was part of someone's fertile imagination. Do these negative charged souls not marvel at special effects in movies, or do they turn to their hapless movie companions and mutter "special effects" or "totally fake"?

And what do people who call "Photoshop," even if correct, actually get out of it? Do they feel informative? Useful? Validated? They are in fact none of these. Annoying perhaps, condescending most certainly. On occasion a fan will link over to snopes.org, a site that has somehow become the definitive spot for debunking claims, urban legends, and Internet rumors. But Snopes itself is run by a retired couple out of California (according to Wikipedia) and as far as I know, nobody stops to ask whether that site has been vetted properly. It is ironic to me that someone can dismiss something on the Internet by referring to something else on the Internet.

For that matter, why in this day and age does anyone expect that the Internet is there to present us with complete reality? We understand that movies, books and theater are laden with fiction, and that our disbelief is to be suspended in order for us to enjoy ourselves. The Internet is a place of both fact and fiction, akin to television in some ways, but we still haven't figured out how to tune our brains properly to that. Perhaps this is the magic behind the Infomercial — it appears to be "informative" but really is a bunch of malarkey (thank you, Joe Biden, for resurrecting that fine word). We're all supposed to be savvy enough to understand this, but obviously there are enough dupes out there to believe anything they are fed.

Now, I can understand the outcry if a "news" organization put out a photoshopped image and expected everyone to accept it at face value. But even our "news" these days often comes packaged with strong biases. The media is starting to understand that people will "buy" what they want to hear. That explains the growing popularity of MSNBC among liberals and FOX News among conservatives. They are the

"Infonewtials" of the modern era.

When it comes to pure laughs, however, maybe the Internet should be put through a less arduous screening, and we should be able to have a good chuckle about something without someone else throwing a wet blanket over it all. I say, save the debunking for important facts and rumors, not for images and memes meant to entertain.

The Internet is, after all, a place where mistakes, like mutations, may be propagated into reality. Recently, I shared an article posted by huffingtonpost.com about a woman in Louisiana who claimed she'd been set on fire by three men, who later scrawled "KKK" on her car. It was truly a horrific story, and I expressed my outrage that such an attack could still occur today. A special "prayer" page had been set up online for the victim, and I included a link to that. Unfortunately, the entire thing turned out to be a tragic fabrication. Evidence soon indicated that the woman in fact had set herself on fire and invented her attackers. Upon learning this, I posted a "retraction" of my earlier post, and expressed pity for the woman who clearly was in need of a "different kind of help" now.

This was a keen lesson in how fake stories can become real in a matter of seconds, but was also an indication of how the Internet ultimately corrects itself. Yes, I took some flak for posting my original outrage. But again, I wonder whether it's fair or realistic to hold someone like me, a private citizen, to a standard of journalistic fact checking. Should I be expected to couch all of my posts with caveats and disclaimers? Should I refrain from sharing anything that might later turn out not to be true? I've given significant thought to this, and concluded that it's better to participate and own up to my own errors than it is to self-censor.

There's another way in which the Internet creates and propagates new things and ideas, even things that are plainly mistakes. Here's an example. When I first started posting online, on occasion I would post a story or anecdote in which the victim turns the tables and "burns" the oppressor back, giving him his due as it were. Fans love a good "got him good" story, and share these liberally with their friends. We all want justice in the world, and examples of wrongdoers getting their comeuppances resonate strongly with all of us. I recall one particular example, of a note left by a co-worker on the office refrigerator - for which I've included the text in the next page for your benefit, since if your eyesight is anything like mine, you most definitely can't read the picture.

DEAR FOOD PILFERERS,

IT'S BEEN APPROXIMATELY ONE MONTH SINCE MY DELICIOUS BROWNIES STARTED RANDOMLY DISAPPEARING, EVEN THOUGH MY NAME WAS CLEARLY AND PROMINENTLY WRITTEN ON THE TUB. I REALLY HOPE YOU ENJOYED THEM AS MUCH AS I WAS UNABLE TO, AS MY 9 YEAR OLD DAUGHTER MADE THEM FOR ME WITH THE HELP OF MY HUSBAND.

OBVIOUSLY, MY PREVIOUS FRIDGE NOTES FELL ON DEAF EARS, SO I DECIDED IT WAS TIME TO TAKE A BIT MORE OF A DIRECT APPROACH. SO, I LEFT AN ANONYMOUS TIP WITH HR, SOMETHING ABOUT THE PROMINENCE OF DRUG USE IN THE COMPANY AND THE POTENTIAL LEGAL RAMIFICATIONS THAT WERE POSSIBLE...YADDA, YADDA YADDA. THAT IS THE REASON WE ALL HAD TO TAKE A RANDOM DRUG TEST YESTERDAY.

OH... I FORGOT TO MENTION... FOR THE LAST TWO WEEKS I HAVE BEEN LACING THE BROWNIES WITH MARIJUANA. NOT A SIGNIFICANT AMOUNT, OBVIOUSLY NOT ENOUGH TO PROVIDE ANY SORT OF EFFECTS, BUT JUST ENOUGH TO SHOW UP ON A DRUG SCREEN.

CHECK. MATE.

I came to understand that this type of story is properly acknowledged with the comment "OWNED,"
as in "she owned him good." Urbandictionary.com
defines it this way:

> **TOTAL AND UNDENIABLE DOMINANCE OF A PERSON, GROUP OF**
> **PEOPLE OR SITUATION AS TO MAKE THEM/IT AKIN TO ONE'S BITCH.**

It really is a colorful word and covers so much of
life's obvious inequities.

I started noticing, however, that some of my fans,
largely young males between the ages of 18 and
25, would comment with the word "PWNED" instead of "OWNED." It occurred too frequently for
it to be a coincidental error. Curious, I asked some
of my younger friends what that meant. Apparently, the term originated in the online game *World
of Warcraft*, which I'm told accounted for a mea-
surable drop in total U.S. productivity after it pre-
miered. In that game, a map designer had created a
typo with the word "owned" and spelled it instead as
"pwned." When the computer defeated a player, instead of saying so-and-so has been "owned" it said,
"has been pwned."

And thus was born a new word, and a fine example of the phenomenon of error replication. If a mistake occurs with regularity, it might well become the
norm. If enough people believe and propagate the

error, it could become gospel. Another example is the term zOMG. I saw this also occur with regularity in my comments, and I had to ask why. Apparently, people mistakenly hit the "z" key instead of the shift key when typing OMG, causing a common error. Enough people did this, and soon it became "it's own thing."

Perhaps this is the real reason the Doubters of the world have their work cut out for them. The Internet is a place where original fiction quickly becomes fact, where mistakes become the norm, and where attribution is nearly impossible.

Betty White is a victim — or perhaps a beneficiary — of this phenomenon. A popular Internet meme, which I also reposted, has her complaining:

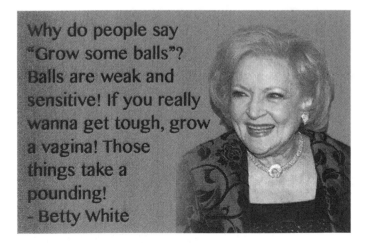

Why do people say "Grow some balls"? Balls are weak and sensitive! If you really wanna get tough, grow a vagina! Those things take a pounding!
- Betty White

Now, according to snopes.com (you see what I did there?), Betty White likely never said this. At least one web administrator source claims that Ms. White wrote him an email, protesting that these were not her words and that she was upset with the attribution. The Doubters postulate that the joke actually belongs to a comedian named Sheng Wang. But here's the thing: It *sounds* like something Betty White would say, and we all wish she really had said it because it makes her all the more "Betty Whitish" to us. People simply are likely to continue to share this and laugh about it until it becomes its own reality.

One of our greatest presidents said it best, in fact:

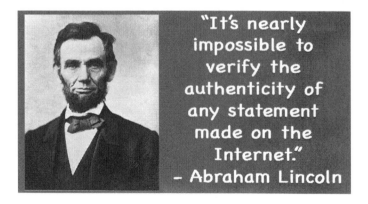

"It's nearly impossible to verify the authenticity of any statement made on the Internet."
– Abraham Lincoln

Use The Source

I don't come up with most of my own images. Nearly all of them come straight from fans, who post them on my wall or send them to me as email attachments through my website. I'll flip through something on the order of a hundred posts — and as many emails — every morning, generally from the day before.

Fans don't always understand that it may be days, weeks or even months before I'll repost something they've shared, even if I really like it. Indeed, it's rare that I'll see something and repost it right away. For starters, there's usually a backlog of things I've been meaning to share. So for something to jump the line, it needs to be particularly compelling.

I'm also admittedly something of a meme hoarder. I've been downloading funny images for nearly two years. Many of them aren't even funny any more, having been beaten to death by so many likes and shares and LOL comments. But I keep them around anyway, tucked away in my virtual chest of funnies. On occasion I'll go back and find a gem or two that makes sense within a particular context or news event, or tickles my fancy because I'm in a mood. Holiday related memes in particular might sit for a whole year before they get hauled out again, like last year's Christmas tree ornaments or Brad's Easter Bunny ears.

I'm also a morning person — a very early morning person — and as a consequence I'm usually up at the crack of dawn reviewing fan submissions. Nobody else would ever see them if I shared them right away. So if something makes me laugh or think, I'll download it and give it a file name that will help me remember what it is later. Or at least that's the idea. Often the naming helps not a whit. I'm looking at a file name "FunnyFromBradGandalf" and have no recollection whatsoever of it, if it's from Brad Gandalf, or if this means Brad found something funny about Gandalf.

It's further apparent to me that the vast majority of these images don't belong to the fans who sent them. They are typically images they found on some other site, or had some other friend send to them. So the best that I can say at any time is "From a fan" — if I even remember that it came from a fan, and not one of my interns as they surfed the Net. Truth be told, by the time I get around to posting the image, I have really no idea where it came from, unless some kind of credit appears as a mark on the image itself. Often certain humor sites add their Facebook URL or website to the image to try and preserve some kind of ownership or claim over it, but as is typically the case, even those sites are at best borrowers of the image.

I commend sites and comics that come up with original content. One of my favorites is Rick Polito, who writes film summaries for a newspaper. Here are some of my favorites of Rick's:

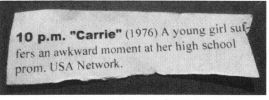

Photo Credit: Rick Polito. Used with Permission

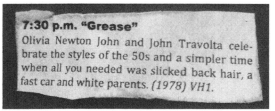

Photo Credit: Rick Polito. Used with Permission

Photo Credit: Rick Polito. Used with Permission

I also really like a Facebook page called "Beware of Images"—which also apparently takes the time to create some original, thought-provoking memes like this one:

Before you judge others or claim any absolute truth, consider that...

...you can see less than 1% of the electromagnetic spectrum and hear less than 1% of the acoustic spectrum. As you read this, you are traveling at 220 kilometres per second across the galaxy. 90% of the cells in your body carry their own microbial DNA and are not "you". The atoms in your body are 99.9999999999999999% empty space and none of them are the ones you were born with, but they all originated in the belly of a star. Human beings have 46 chromosomes, 2 less than the common potato. The existence of the rainbow depends on the conical photoreceptors in your eyes; to animals without cones, the rainbow does not exist. So you don't just look at a rainbow, you create it. This is pretty amazing, especially considering that all the beautiful colors you see represent less than 1% of the electromagnetic spectrum.

Or frankly hilarious ones like these:

Photo Credit: Sergio Toporek. Used with Permission.

Photo Credit: Mariel Clayton. Used with Permission.

But these are the exceptions. Most content on the Internet appears to have oozed forth from some primordial and undifferentiated goop. This makes identifying the original source of an image on the Internet damned near impossible. Even in the drafting of this book, when I wanted to use a particularly funny image, I have had my interns move heaven and earth to try and find out who really owned it, verify that as best as they could, and then get written permission to put it in the book. But after all this, I am dubious of many claims of ownership and rights to license.

Despite my best efforts to give proper attribution, fans and page administrators of other sites have taken issue with me. For example, on occasion I will read comments and a fan will simply write words like "9gag" or "Reddit" in the comment stream. I am not a user of sites beyond the ones I post on (Facebook, Twitter, Pinterest, and on rare occasion Google+). So I had to ask around about what these sites were, and then I paid them a quick visit.

It turns out there are whole humor sites out there where fans generate memes and share them with one another, and on some vote them up or down. To quote Betty White, "It seems like an awful waste of time." I'm sure these sites have their avid followings, but I already have my hands full looking through my own wall posts from fans without having to look at more.

I figure if something is particularly funny on "Reddit" someone will probably post it to my wall, and I can get it there. Nor does it bother me that some other page posted it first. Being "first" in the Internet is like being the first runner to round the curve in a race. People may notice you momentarily, but then you're just another runner with the pack, trying to make it to the finish line.

Speaking of being "first," I've also noticed that many of my posts will begin their comment streams with some fan posting the word "FIRST!" There are a number of amusing things about this. There's no prize for being first, so I'm not exactly sure what the point of the comment is. I sometime wonder if there are people out there who sit watching their screen for one of my posts, just so they can claim to be first. I suppose it's the same mentality that causes people to camp out for iPhones or concert tickets.

Moreover, the poster can never really be sure they are first, because they are competing for that position with tens of thousands of other readers. Someone can probably type "lol" faster than "FIRST!" making the "FIRST!" look rather foolish sitting there in second place for all the world to see. And in any case, the "FIRST!" commenters subject themselves to significant ridicule even if they manage to be first, with sneering responses such as "Wow, Walter, you're first. Do you want a friggin' cookie? Loser."

I've had some fun with this "FIRST!" phenomenon, readying myself to type "FIRST!" in the comment box as soon as my post appears. I know, it's cheating, but it's to underscore the silliness of the process. I once got over 50 likes just for posting my own "FIRST!" comment (yes, I actually go back and look to see who's paying attention). Now, the other day, I actually tried this ruse but came in second. That got me steamed, looking at my "First" declaration squeezed sadly into second place by some hack. Then I remembered that it was my page. I simply clicked "hide" on the comment above mine.

Problem solved, I'm still the winner!

But back to the question of sources. As I noted earlier in this book, time and again, I've fought a battle between the need to get something out quickly (to remain topical) and the need to verify something's authenticity (to remain credible). I rely on my fans to provide me with content, and I have no real idea where they get their information or their images.

Newsrooms face this problem every day of their existence from listener tips, but I tend to face it most during disasters and elections. During Hurricane Sandy, for example, I took it upon myself, somewhat naively, to try and provide information and resources about the storm. I encouraged fans to send in photos of storm damage, thinking that this might help motivate other fans to donate money to relief efforts out of sympathy. Similarly, I encouraged fans to send me election-related stories, particularly if they were in long polling lines or their machines did not record their votes accurately.

The problem, of course, was that some of the photos I began to receive were obviously fabricated — "shopped" as it were, or taken from another storm while claiming to be current. Some of the information I received was quite apparently inaccurate or misleading. Twice on Election Day I had to take down posts that listed "hotline" numbers which actually were partisan in nature. "Storm coverage" photos showing sharks swimming inland in New Jersey were dubious. Reports of power outages and power plant explosions couldn't be verified.

There really isn't a good answer to getting sources right, particularly since my outfit here consists of me, Brad and our interns. We can't spend our time fact checking everything that pushes past our emails or my wall. And realistically speaking, I can't be expected to provide credit, let alone obtain permission, with respect to each image, meme or quote I put up on my page. In this sense Facebook, Tumblr and Pinterest run smack into copyright laws that no one has figured out how, or even whether, to enforce.

Perhaps the best solution is to simply not take our "Internet" sources or information too seriously. During Hurricane Sandy, many of my fans were spending their energy imploring me not to post pictures that may not have been taken that day or may have been "shopped." Out of exasperation, I posted this image, but emphasized that due to the high number of fake images out there, I had verified it first with Fox News:

Now, to be fair and balanced, on election night, I also posted: "MSNBC called the election for Obama, but that was back in October."

Epic Fail, Epic Win

I appreciate failure. Failure means that an attempt was made, and a lesson can be learned. As long as we're alive after the effort, there is a chance for success the next time around. As a friend sometimes says to me, "That which does not kill us pisses the hell out of us."

A "fail" can be small or big. We appreciate the special kind of humor that small fails can bring: a sign advertising a ham special for Hanukkah; autocorrects that turn innocuous texts from family members into erotic messages; a Facebook profile of a woman next to Leonard Nimoy, with the caption "Biggest *Star Wars* fan ever!" The small failures bring us together because each of us experiences them regularly and can relate. They are reminders of our own tendency to make mistakes while hoping no one else sees them.

When failures happen to famous people, they remind us that we're all human, and that we shouldn't take failure as an indictment of who we are, or who we might become.

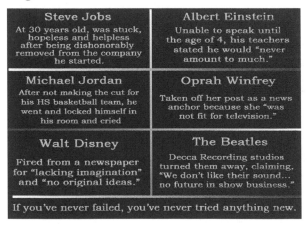

Steve Jobs	Albert Einstein
At 30 years old, was stuck, hopeless and helpless after being dishonorably removed from the company he started.	Unable to speak until the age of 4, his teachers stated he would "never amount to much."
Michael Jordan	**Oprah Winfrey**
After not making the cut for his HS basketball team, he went and locked himself in his room and cried	Taken off her post as a news anchor because she "was not fit for television."
Walt Disney	**The Beatles**
Fired from a newspaper for "lacking imagination" and "no original ideas."	Decca Recording studios turned them away, claiming, "We don't like their sound... no future in show business."

If you've never failed, you've never tried anything new.

"Epic" fails speak to us on a somewhat different level. By epic, I mean something with grand scope and grand design. "Grand" of course is all in the mind of the dreamer; something can be epic even if the dreamer is no hero. To be epic is an attempt, even by the common person, to achieve or experience the inconceivable. We recognize when others have pushed their own limits and, as a consequence, rendered their choices and actions epic. Thus, a rafting trip with friends down a river can be epic, especially if it is their first time paddling. An all night bender can turn epic for all its unexpected twists and turns, especially if someone winds up sharing a jail cell with a transvestite hooker.

So what, then, is an epic fail, and why do we love them so? We've all seen clips of the first attempts to build flying machines of all kinds. We wince as these contraptions flap and tumble and crash, and then oddly we smile, even as we avert our gaze. We know they have failed, usually miserably, and yet we admire them for the effort. This is in part because we know how that story ends — in the case of those early machines, with a triumphant first flight by the Wright Brothers. It's also undeniably hilarious to watch others give it their all, only to fall flat on their faces. It's a form of schadenfreude — made popular by the musical *Avenue Q* — to experience "happiness at the misery of others."

We've all seen those hapless contenders on talent shows who really have no talent whatsoever, singing and dancing as if they were born to be in the spotlight. Assuming they have winning attitudes — i.e., they are trying out because they really DO want to be the next "American Idol" — a part of us still admires them, even as inside a little part of us dies as we beg, "Oh stop. Please, please, please stop."

Websites such as Fail Blog have begun to capture

and agglomerate many of these epic failures. Looking through some of these, it occurs to me that there are some common threads among them:

We really can't believe what we're seeing. A hallmark of epic failure is a sense of disbelief at what we're witnessing. This disbelief arises in part from the conservative, cautious nature within most of us, which would simply never permit such an attempt in the first instance. This helps explain the popularity of shows like *Wipe Out* and *Jackass*. How many of us would ever attempt these feats?

We watch it over and over again. Unlike most jokes or funny images, we watch epic failure clips on repeat. Repeat views probably account for more than half of the total views. We also show our friends those same dreadful moments, so that they, too, can watch it over and over. In fact, some of the most epic failure clips have been "remixed" so that the "fail" repeats again and again and again. The editor simply knows and understands that this is what we've tuned in to see.

We are evil and going to hell. Whenever I post something that shouldn't be funny but somehow people can't help but laugh, I receive a number of posts along the lines of, "That was in terrible taste, George. But I love it!" or "I'm going to hell for laughing." We are all taught that we shouldn't mock others for their misfortune, so when it happens, we have to admit that a little part of each of us is evil. I mean, try not to laugh at this meme. I actually received a comment from an angry fan after posting this, to which I responded with a joke actually used in the script for *Allegiance*. Here's the exchange:

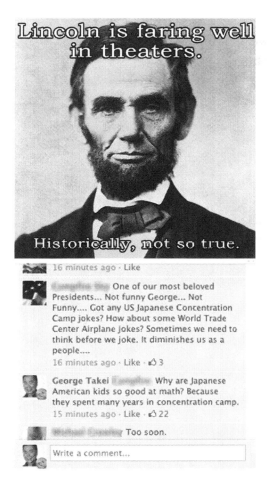

16 minutes ago · Like

One of our most beloved Presidents... Not funny George... Not Funny.... Got any US Japanese Concentration Camp jokes? How about some World Trade Center Airplane jokes? Sometimes we need to think before we joke. It diminishes us as a people....
16 minutes ago · Like · 👍 3

George Takei   Why are Japanese American kids so good at math? Because they spent many years in concentration camp.
15 minutes ago · Like · 👍 22

Too soon.

Write a comment...

Even more potent than the epic fail is the epic win. To explain this, let me first say a few words about "winning." Unfortunately, "winning" generally took a bit of a beating when a certain douchebag began using it as his favorite hashtag on Twitter after being fired from his hit television show. But once that awful smoke cleared, a "win" again resumed its proper place on the Internet.

A "win" is not only the opposite of a fail, it is truly the happy end point of many failures. Parenting is a good example. Most new parents, well intentioned as they are and fresh from every sort of parenting seminar or course imaginable, maintain a deep and abiding suspicion that they are doing it wrong. This fear tends to recede the more children people have, which might account for why there are so many large families. It's no surprise that instances of parenting "wins" have proven to be some of the most popular of my memes.

Other parenting wins include pictures of how parents turned a child's wheelchair into an ice cream truck or a bulldozer or a tie-fighter for Halloween. These examples prove that parents can be heroes with a bit of imagination and effort. After all, if the parents of these disabled kids can make their day, what's your excuse?

Another kind of "win" occurs when people are simply unafraid to be who they are and truly "go for it." I've posted images that run the gamut, everything from a guy dressed as Darth Vader riding a unicycle down a busy street to an unabashedly "fabulous" little boy posing with his arms up as if already cast in a Fosse musical. I've noted that when the "win" falls outside of generally accepted behavior, it's often accompanied by the words "Haters gonna hate" — which is really a rallying cry for the misfits of the world to step forward and break some rules.

Another popular type of "win" is really better described as a "burn" or an "owned" (or a "pwned" if you are a gamer). These wins put bullies in their place, or turn the tables on the intolerant or bigoted using their own language. For example, when Dr. Laura Schlessinger infamously declared back in the 1990s that homosexuals were a "mistake of nature," she received a letter which later became a viral hit when it made its way onto the Internet:

DEAR DR. LAURA,

[...] I HAVE LEARNED A GREAT DEAL FROM YOUR SHOW. [...] WHEN SOMEONE TRIES TO DEFEND THE HOMOSEXUAL LIFESTYLE, FOR EXAMPLE, I SIMPLY REMIND HIM THAT LEVITICUS 18:22 CLEARLY STATES IT TO BE AN ABOMINATION. END OF DEBATE. I DO NEED SOME ADVICE FROM YOU, HOWEVER, REGARDING SOME OF THE SPECIFIC LAWS AND HOW TO BEST FOLLOW THEM. [...]

- I WOULD LIKE TO SELL MY DAUGHTER INTO SLAVERY, AS

SANCTIONED IN *EXODUS 21:7*. IN THIS DAY AND AGE, WHAT DO
YOU THINK WOULD BE A FAIR PRICE FOR HER? [...]

- *LEV. 25:44* STATES THAT I MAY INDEED POSSESS SLAVES,
BOTH MALE AND FEMALE, PROVIDED THEY ARE PURCHASED FROM
NEIGHBORING NATIONS. A FRIEND OF MINE CLAIMS THAT THIS AP-
PLIES TO MEXICANS, BUT NOT CANADIANS. CAN YOU CLARIFY? WHY
CAN'T I OWN CANADIANS? [...]

YOUR DEVOTED DISCIPLE AND ADORING FAN.

This exchange was so "winning" that Aaron Sor-
kin adopted it for use in *The West Wing* in a famous
exchange between Jeb Bartlett and a conservative
"Doctor" opposed to gay rights.

So what makes an epic win? Keep in mind, the
"epicness" of the quest for a win need not be in ab-
solute terms. Epic is all in the mind of the attempter.
Thus, one of my most popular links was to a story of
a small town hero, David Andrews, who played for
his high school basketball team outside of Memphis.
David has Down Syndrome and didn't have many
opportunities on the court, but when fate (and his
coach) called upon him to step up, he did in a major
way, scoring three point jumpers to rival the best of
the pros. This led his coach to put David in as a start-
er who helped lead the team to the county champion-
ship. It brings tears to my eyes just to recall watching
that clip[1].

---

1   www.abcnews.go.com/WNT/video/syndrome-player-star-15761771

In this way, many of the best epic wins defy the odds and strip us of our cynicism.

A win turns epic when it touches upon our deepest hopes and dazzles us with its sweep. This explains the attraction of movies such as *The Hunger Games, Harry Potter, Lord of the Rings* or *Star Wars*, when an unknown hero or heroine saves the planet or even the whole galaxy. Within each of us is the secret wish that we were born for greater things, have superhero powers, or simply haven't been given the chance yet to defeat the forces of darkness. The online role-play gaming industry is built entirely around the notion of epic wins, giving skinny, awkward young males (and not a few females) a world to imagine beyond cubicles and acne.

My successful ventures on the Internet have been described by the press as an epic win for someone of my age and background, but I like to break it down a bit. I admit, I have had my share of "winning" moments that brought a lot of joy.

One in particular stands out, from a post in April:

FRIENDS, I'M THRILLED TO SHARE THIS NEWS WITH YOU TODAY. AS ANNOUNCED AT EMERALD CITY COMICON, WHERE I'M APPEARING THIS WEEKEND, PARAMOUNT PICTURES HAS GREEN-LIT A NEW STAR TREK MOVIE ENTITLED EXCELSIOR IN WHICH I WILL PLAY THE CAPTAIN. THIS ANNOUNCEMENT IS PART OF PARAMOUNT STUDIO'S 100TH-YEAR ANNIVERSARY CAMPAIGN. THE STUDIO HAS ACKNOWLEDGED THE FAN ENTHUSIASM FOR THIS CONCEPT EVER SINCE

I appeared in command of the vessel in The Undiscovered Country. J.J. Abrams will direct, with Roberto Orci again writing the screenplay.

My co-star in Allegiance, Paolo Montalban, has been cast opposite me to play the mercurial "Agha," the grandson of Khan (played by Ricardo Montalban in the second Star Trek movie). Also featured are Gilbert Gottfried (playing a wily Ferengi First Officer) and Lisa Lampanelli (as a Bajoran security officer).

More to come on this breaking story soon. Thanks again for the years of support, and I'll see you on the Bridge of Excelsior.

This news was greeted by cheers and applause across my fan base — except for those who realized the date it was published: April 1st. Yes, I'd pulled off one of the most epic April Fools' Day pranks ever, with tens of thousands of fans duped. Not even the improbable casting of Gilbert and Lisa dissuaded some of fans who were so ready to see me take the helm. Even to this day, I'm asked when the movie will be coming out. Alas, it is not. But at least I've got this epic win under my belt.

Oh Myyy!

242

Takei 3.0

So that's the gist of it, friends. There's probably much more I could say, but I've rattled on enough for now. It's been an astonishing two years on the Internet for me, and I'm still just taking it all in.

Who knew that the World Wide Web would be ready to welcome me so warmly? Anyone who says that the Golden Years are anything less than that should give me a call. Or better yet, drop me a note on my Facebook Wall. I'm more likely to respond there.

While these two years have flown by, I have no doubt that the coming years will be just as eye-popping, challenging and rewarding for this former helmsman of the *Enterprise*.

I've got big plans to bring my community of fans

even closer together, and to dig a bit deeper on the pressing questions of the day, even as we remember to keep things lighthearted so as not to take ourselves too seriously. I'm calling it Takei 3.0.

So stay tuned, friends, and stay engaged. As this world grows ever more connected, as our media grows ever more social, I'll be there, laughing alongside you as the naughty gay Asian uncle you wish you had.

With that, I'm going to leave you with one last cat meme, below. The cat somehow reminds me of my husband.

Hope you don't mind me being catty, Brad. Love you.

-- George

Made in the USA
Lexington, KY
14 May 2013